A PHILOSOPHY OF PLAY

NRPA Recreation and Park Perspective Collection

edited by Dr. Diana R. Dunn
Director of Research
National Recreation and Park Association

Education through Play	Curtis, H.	$19.00
Education through Recreation	Jacks, L.	$13.00
Education by Plays and Games	Johnson, G.	$15.00
The New Leisure Challenges for the Schools	Lies, E.	$17.00
Play in Education	Lee, J.	$25.00
Play and Mental Health	Davis, J.	$15.00
Education through Recreation	Johnson, G.	$10.00
The Practical Conduct of Play	Curtis, H.	$19.00
The Play Movement	Rainwater, C.	$21.00
The Play Movement and its Significance	Curtis, H.	$19.00
Playground Technique and Playcraft	Leland, A. & L.	$17.00
American Playgrounds	Mero, E.	$17.00
Leisure in the Modern World	Burns, C.	$15.00
The Threat of Leisure	Cutten, G.	$12.00
The Normal Course of Play	NRA	$16.00
The Education of the Whole Man	Jacks, L.	$12.00
The Challenge of Leisure	Pack, A.	$14.00
Off the Job Living	Romney, G.	$15.00
A Philosophy of Play	Gulick, L.	$16.00
Europe at Play	Weir, L.	$45.00
Music in American Life	Zanzig, A.	$28.00
Music in Institutions	Van de Wall, W.	$35.00
The First County Park System	Kelsey, F.	$15.00
County Parks	NRA	$14.00
Central Park—First Annual Report	New York	$14.00
The Spirit of Youth and the City Streets	Addams, J.	$12.00
Annals March 1910	AAP&SS	$16.00
Municipalization of Play and Recreation	Fulk, J.	$10.00
Luther Halsey Gulick	Dorgan, E.	$14.00
Constructive and Preventive Philanthropy	Lee, J.	$15.00

order from:

McGrath Publishing Company
Washington, D.C.

A PHILOSOPHY OF PLAY

BY
LUTHER HALSEY GULICK, M.D.

WITH A FOREWORD
BY
JOSEPH LEE

McGrath Publishing Company

&

NATIONAL RECREATION AND PARK ASSOCIATION
WASHINGTON, D.C.

COPYRIGHT, 1920, BY
CHARLOTTE VETTER GULICK

Library of Congress Cataloging in Publication Data

Gulick, Luther Halsey, 1865-1918.
  A philosophy of play.

    1. Play. I. Title.
BF717.G94 1972   155.2   72-1948
ISBN 0-8434-0440-X

FOREWORD

If you want to know what a child is, study his play; if you want to affect what he shall be, direct the form of play. These are the principles enunciated in the first chapter of this book, and abundantly enforced in those that follow.

To those of us who are interested in the recreation movement, the book comes as the last message of the master; to all Doctor Gulick's fellow citizens it is the legacy of an American pioneer in the vitally important field of education. It has behind it twenty years of study and experiment. It is the fruit of observation, not of the photographic sort, but carried on with an uncanny X-ray power of intuition, and yet without losing that "innocence of the eye" —the power of seeing what is there, not what you expect to see—so necessary to fresh discovery.

The authoritative value of Doctor Gulick's opinions may be partly judged from his practical experience as an innovator. I suppose that in laying down, when he was teaching at the International Y. M. C. A. Training-School in

Springfield, the principles out of which the game of basket-ball was there evolved, he became the only man who has ever through deliberate action added to our too short list of major sports. His New York Public Schools Athletic League, a pioneer institution, has grown and prospered. His Camp Fire Girls represent a long step toward the discovery of the girl. The Playground and Recreation Association of America, of which he was a principal founder, has led in the development of play and recreation in this country. His teaching has, through the Y. M. C. A. and other organizations, been a great influence in the social and physical training of the American armies in the great war, and has profoundly influenced the morale of the men. His death resulted from personal devotion to this object in Y. M. C. A. work in France.

Doctor Gulick's heresy, in describing Froebel as having evolved his educational methods without first observing the child's actual play, which, in fact, Froebel spent fifteen years in studying, and in criticising Froebel's games as not actually played by the children outside the kindergarten—ignoring Froebel's whole intention, which was not to invent new children's games but to utilize the form of children's games to carry their education on beyond—will be forgiven by all true Froebellians, who will recognize in Doctor Gulick a most potent ally in the promulgation of some of their dearest principles.

It is most fortunate that Miss Anna L. von der Osten, who worked with Doctor Gulick in the original preparation of this manuscript, has generously given her time to the final editing of the manuscript and to the careful reading of the proof. Every reader of the book will be indebted to her for this effective service.

The book is not for physical educators alone, but for fathers and mothers, school-teachers, social workers, and lovers of children and grown children everywhere.

JOSEPH LEE.

CONTENTS

		PAGE
FOREWORD	. . . .	v
INTRODUCTION	. . . .	xi

CHAPTER		
I.	THE EXTENT OF THE PLAY INTEREST .	1
II.	SEPARATION VS. CONCENTRATION . . .	12
III.	HUNTING AND FIGHTING PLAYS . . .	16
IV.	PLAYING HOUSE	33
V.	FIRE PLAY	49
VI.	TOYS—CONSTRUCTION AND OWNERSHIP .	67
VII.	MASCULINE AND FEMININE DIFFERENCES	83
VIII.	THE PLAY OF ANIMALS	99
IX.	THE PLAY OF ADULTS	113
X.	THE PLAY OF SUBNORMAL CHILDREN .	128
XI.	PLAY PROGRESSION	141
XII.	PLAY AND PHYSICAL GROWTH . . .	155

CONTENTS

CHAPTER		PAGE
XIII.	Play and Education	171
XIV.	Play and Moral Growth	184
XV.	Instinct and Tradition in Play	197
XVI.	Play and Our Changing Civilization	211
XVII.	Play and the Modern City	224
XVIII.	Direction and Control in Play—Playgrounds	230
XIX.	Play and Democracy	243
XX.	Play, the Pursuit of the Ideal	266
	Index	283

INTRODUCTION

My professional connection with physical training, athletics, and games dating from 1886 to 1906, gave opportunity and incentive for the study of play in many of its aspects. I was led to ask many questions. Why do boys give to play so much greater earnestness and zest than they give to work? Why do Americans play baseball and the English cricket? Why have women never had a great team game? Why are the Anglo-Saxons the only peoples who have developed team games, polo and lacrosse excepted? Is it by heredity or environment that boys play fighting games and girls play with dolls? What is play? How are play customs formed? How are they passed on through the generations? Can the underlying forces of play be so well understood that they may be applied in other directions, in education or morals? What light does a study of play throw on the nature of the player?

To the answering of questions such as these the bulk of my available time and attention was given for over twenty years. In this volume my aim is to give to others what I can of my conclusions and of the data upon which they rest. I have not hesitated, however, to state some conclusions, the data for which are not given here.

In studying play I have come to believe that it affords the best and most profitable way of studying humankind itself, both individuals and races. Play consists of that which people do when they have food, shelter, and clothing, are rested and free from worry, when the physical compulsions of life are removed temporarily and the spirit is free to search for its own satisfactions. Then man is at his best. The pursuit of food, shelter, clothing, and safety is in the main the means to life; but these things are not the end for which life seems to exist. For this reason I believe that man is better revealed by his play, or by the use he makes of his leisure time, than by any one other index.

The way in which the spirit of man works when it is free from the shackles of compulsion is not accounted for by any of the present-day systems of psychology. In play we see the action of great desires, operating with indifference to consciousness or intelligence; the intellect is used as a tool with which to accomplish ends, rather than as a guide. Bergson and the pragmatists seem to have come nearer this conception than have the psychologists.

The origin and development of gangs and team games among boys similarly present facts that do not seem to harmonize with the views of contemporary sociologists. Gumplowitz alone discusses the relations of the individual to the group, the growth of morals versus rights, in a way consistent with the facts as I have observed them.

I am stating my conclusions at the start, for few readers will be equally interested in all parts of these studies, and yet the conclusions themselves may shed light upon the various parts and may thus serve as a guide.

I have not neglected the literature of play, having read, I think, all that has been carefully written on the subject in English, French, and German. Most of these contributions seem to me to be without deep value because: 1. The writer had formed his theories before he had secured his facts, and hence bent the facts to conform. 2. He was acquainted with but a few aspects of the facts. 3. He recorded facts, but did not attempt to interpret them. 4. In most cases the writers on play and sport have not sufficient knowledge to see the essential facts. The students of play, as I have studied them, have spent far more time at the desk than in watching players. Because the conclusions set forth in this book are based in the main on the first-hand observation or experience of facts, I quote authority but little.

CONCLUSIONS

I. My first conclusion has been stated already in part. The individual is more completely revealed in play than in any one other way; and conversely, play has a greater shaping power over the character and nature of man than has any one other activity. A man shows what he really is when he is free to do what he chooses, and if a person can be influenced so that his highest aspirations—which are followed when he is free to pursue his ideals—are a gain, then character is being shaped profoundly.

II. A people most truly reveals itself in the character of its pleasures. The pleasures of a people are not the sum of the pleasures of the individuals who compose that people, just as the psychology of the crowd is quite different from the psychology of the individuals composing the crowd.

Conversely, the manner of its pleasures is the most character-determining force within a people. Chinese characteristics are not biologically inherited, as we know by the results of cross adaptation. Chinese characteristics are race tradition inheritances passed on predominantly by the plays and games of the Chinese children. Embedded here in the amber of tradition is the quintessence of that which is Chinese. It passes to the child by the turn of an ancient phrase, the mode of seeing the world as indicated in a century-old story, or the muscular movements of a ceremonial greeting. I doubt if any of us understand the feelings of the Orientals who did not as children play Oriental games in an Oriental atmosphere, with Oriental children.

III. It is an impression which has been growing during my years of observation, that the individual is more an agent in life than a directing force. It seems that certain great desires engulf the individual, directing his will, his purposes, to their own ends, with but slight regard for the benefit of the individual himself. These desires come in great waves, growing larger and farther apart as the years pass from infancy to old age. Each of these great waves or tides of desire raises the level of the psychic range and power of the individual, and makes the next one possible. These waves also in a general way seem to mark the successive periods of progress of prehistoric man. In this sense each individual recapitulates the history of his kind, both in individual growth and in social relations.

LUTHER HALSEY GULICK.

A PHILOSOPHY OF PLAY

A Philosophy of Play

CHAPTER I

THE EXTENT OF THE PLAY INTEREST

IN the spring of the year occurs a series of events to which more space is given in many of the newspapers which record the world's happenings than would be given to a State election. In normal times when the baseball games between the large cities of America begin, the reports of their Saturday scores take precedence over almost all other news in the minds of hundreds of thousands of men. Men and boys will stand in groups miles away from the game, watching, throughout the afternoon, while the scores are flashed upon a screen. This enthusiasm is out of all proportion to the actual utility of the game. A similar interest was shown in the Jeffries-Johnson fight. All over the United States men were discussing it, men who did not see it when it took place, whose lives and business it could never touch in any possible way. And this discussion continued for over a year. An unusual and apparently uncalled-for interest of this kind seems to need some explanation.

In the fall the great college football games begin. They occupy but slightly less space in the newspapers than do the intercity baseball contests. But their effect in the college world is even greater. Before an important game each college holds football rallies. In many universities more students are present at these rallies than at any other student meeting of the year. They learn songs and cheers; they encourage the players. On the day of the game thirty or forty thousand spectators may frequently be seen in the bleachers watching a football match between two of the large Eastern colleges, or two of the Middle West State universities. At the first important play the entire crowd arises and remains standing, breathless, lest a play be lost. The student bands lead in the college songs and the cheer leaders wear their throats hoarse in the effort to direct enthusiasm. A man on the field is knocked out; his substitute is put on. The students cheer for both men by name, but the man who is removed from play is frequently carried off in tears, which no one thinks for a moment of attributing to the pain of any wounds he may have sustained. He is heart-broken for one reason only—because he is out of the game.

A friend who witnessed one of the great games in which Chicago University lost the Western Championship says that she never had seen such compelling enthusiasm as filled the students. After the defeat there was a moment's silence, then a cheer was given by the team for their victorious opponents, and then a thousand young men and women broke spontaneously into the Alma Mater and marched off the field with the band playing. Fully one-third of them were crying from the nervous excitement of the occasion. It was not merely college loyalty that prompted this demonstration. A victory in debate would have aroused enthusiasm, but not in an equal measure. A convincing proof of the superiority of their institution to all others in scholarship—the supposedly real test of a university—would elicit barely a cheer. The spirit shown in the game goes much deeper, and seems sufficiently significant to demand consideration.

Playing baseball on the streets of New York is forbidden by a city ordinance. Yet every day during the spring a large proportion of the boys brought before the judge of the Children's Court are there for the crime of playing ball.

4 A PHILOSOPHY OF PLAY

The black-robed judge questions them from behind a high desk; a big policeman stands near to give testimony. The boys are in the position of lawbreakers, yet most of them are decent, respectable boys, frequently very young and much frightened. There is another game called "Cat," which consists in striking a pointed stick, with the end in view of sending it a certain distance in a given direction. It is not a very thrilling game, apparently, yet it furnishes sometimes as many as one-seventh of the total arrests of the court. The boys have risked arrest to play it.

In one of the crowded city playgrounds of New York, where the boys were so close that it was impossible to see through the group for ten yards in any direction, several games of ball were going on. Every time the ball was hit, it was either lost in the crowd or it rolled under the iron railing, and had to be tossed in by a boy outside. Clearly, no real game was possible; and yet the boys were attempting it. In a near-by street the sidewalks were covered with baseball games. Here stood a batter, a few yards away a pitcher, and close behind the pitcher was the catcher for another game. There were seven games of ball going on at the same time on the sidewalk on one side of a

EXTENT OF THE PLAY INTEREST

single block. Regardless of cars, trucks, and automobiles, the boys dodged across the street after the ball whenever the batter was fortunate enough to hit it.

Suddenly, far up the street, one of the games stopped, then the next, then the next. The boys slipped away by twos and threes into alleys and cellar-doors. A street-car went by with a policeman on the front platform. After he had passed the boys reappeared and the games went on. Those boys were not lawbreakers at heart. Their mothers and fathers were sitting on the stoops watching their play, and approving it. The games were going on under every conceivable difficulty. An instinct strong enough to impel boys to play baseball under conditions like these is worthy of attention.

A gang to which I belonged as a boy, was called the Boys' Jolly Club. We spent a large part of our free time hunting English sparrows. There is a delight in shooting a sparrow, pulling off its feathers, cooking and eating it, half-done, that is not found in all the food from mother's pantry. We would also go through the woods to hunt squirrels, with a little .22-caliber rifle, ten, twelve, fourteen hours in succession. When we ate our lunch we finished it as quickly as possible, because we might get another squirrel.

We did not need the squirrels. I did indeed devise a kind of justification for myself—I always made a point of saving the skin and getting some one to eat the squirrel. But I did not need the skins and I did not need the food. Yet I had this desire to hunt, although my feelings about hunting are not particularly strong.

These feelings are not confined to children. I have never yet, day or night, gone by the docks on the Hudson River without seeing men sitting there waiting for fish to bite. There are little boys and gray-haired men. I have gone up close to the docks at ten or eleven o'clock at night, and even then have found some individuals fishing. No doubt there are times in the day when people do not fish, but I have never discovered such times. I have never seen it rain hard enough to clear the docks of men who were fishing. One of my friends was a Springfield banker. Once when he had a day's vacation he came to a small lake near our house and sat in the rain all day fishing. He got a little string of perch averaging five inches. Yet he had a glorious time. Most of the men who fish on the Hudson are not doing it because they need the fish. They are doing it from mere love of fishing.

The term play covers a group of activities as

EXTENT OF THE PLAY INTEREST 7

wide as the scope of human life. It goes even further than human life, for animals also play. Among human beings play is part of the activity of babies, children, young people, and adults. Play has always been of interest to all mankind. Yet there is a sense in which the conscious interest in play is new. There is now a well-established play movement throughout the United States, and, indeed, throughout the civilized world. China, India, and other Eastern countries have set apart play centres. One of the first cities in the United States to establish playgrounds was Boston. After Boston had tried playgrounds for twenty-six years, the Massachusetts legislature passed an act requiring all municipalities having 10,000 or more inhabitants to vote on the question of establishing and maintaining playgrounds with adequate supervision.

Chicago has probably made a larger single appropriation for recreation than any one city. In a little more than two years Chicago set aside $10,000,000 for small parks and playgrounds, and since that time millions have been spent in developing, administering, and enlarging the system. Their recreation centres provide indoor and outdoor gymnasiums for both men and women; sand gardens and wading pools for the smaller children; ball fields for the boys and men; outdoor swimming-pools, restaurants, libraries, neighborhood club-rooms, and an auditorium. All this is paid for by the city, not by private philanthropy. And the use of these grounds has shown their need. The places have become neighborhood centres in the most promising sense. It is said that aldermen in Chicago lose all popularity with their constituents unless they secure playgrounds in their wards.

In 1907, 57 cities reported that they were conducting playgrounds, 54 of these having 836 grounds. The annual cost of maintenance for 44 of the cities reporting was $904,102. In 1918 reports compiled by the Playground and Recreation Association of America showed that 504 cities conducted work under the direction of paid leaders at an expenditure of $6,659,-600.84. In addition 108 cities reported that their schools were used as social centres.

A movement of this kind demands attention. Temptation is strong to continue with the enumeration of special instances of the splendid growth and deepening social significance of the playground movement throughout the country; but enough has been said to dissipate the impression that it is merely a local or transient fad. It is an awakening on the part of our citi-

EXTENT OF THE PLAY INTEREST

zens to an hitherto almost unrecognized responsibility. What this responsibility is, and why it exists, and what there is in our modern life which has awakened us to it are questions of vital importance.

In the succeeding chapters I shall take up a survey of some of the universal forms of children's plays, the hunting and fighting plays, the shelter plays, the plays of ownership, doll play, playing with toys, and fire play. This is not an exhaustive list of the plays of children, but it is sufficiently representative to show the forces present in play. Certain important forms of play will be omitted altogether or treated briefly. Rhythmical play and festivals will be treated elsewhere, and for that reason are omitted here. Team plays will be discussed only so far as is necessary for the understanding of other topics. The consideration of the playground movement must be omitted, as it is a subject which might easily require a book by itself. Only those phases of it will be considered here which relate directly to the theory of play, such as the problem of play direction.

In the treatment of the various forms of play I shall discuss the survival value, from the evolutionary standpoint, of the feelings involved in play, and the extent to which those feelings are still of use. I shall then take up a brief consideration of the play of animals, the play of adults, and the play of subnormal children, tracing in each case the relation which play bears to the life of the individual. The relations of various plays to one another and to the physical, mental, and moral life of the individual will be discussed with special reference to pedagogical implications to be derived from a study of spontaneous plays of children. The part taken by instinct and by tradition in play, and the effect which play has in preserving the social inheritance of the race, will also be considered in this connection.

The final problems discussed relate to the position of play in modern life. The conditions of our civilization are changing; modern industry has affected the home, the school, the city. The problem of play is in many ways very different from what it was fifty years ago. Play has its relations to the modern city, industry, school, to the modern home. It has also close relations to the ideal which is being tested to-day in America, the ideal of democracy. All these questions must be considered in a theory of play.

There is still one other aspect of the subject —the relation which the spirit of play may bear to all life. Play is more than a name applied to a given list of activities; it is an attitude which may pervade every activity. Play has sometimes been used in this sense in connection with artistic achievement in discussions of æsthetic theories; and it may also be used in connection with all work worth doing. Play as free expression of the self, as the pursuit of the ideal, has direct bearing on the ultimate questions of reality and worth. The spirit of play has value as a philosophy of life.

CHAPTER II

SEPARATION VS. CONCENTRATION

IN order that children over six or seven years old may play wholesomely, good leadership is practically essential. Such leadership is of even greater importance than the playground itself or the play apparatus. A competent leader may secure good results with an exceedingly meagre outfit of play materials and with very limited play space; whereas playgrounds and such play materials as swings, chutes, bats, and balls, used without wise leadership, are frequently productive of evil rather than of good. Directed play is the first requirement for children of the "game" age.

The playground is a device by which a single leader can effectively control the play of a large number of children. It is an aggregating plan, and actual experience has shown that children playing in large groups must have competent persons to lead and supervise them, otherwise the larger and more disorderly boys in the neighborhood make the playground intolerable by day and, in some cases, a positive menace by night.

SEPARATION VS. CONCENTRATION 13

Babies and little children under six years of age, however, present an entirely different problem. It is undesirable to have very small children gathered together in large numbers, and it is unnecessary that their play should be directed. Their first need is suitable space and things to play with. A sand pile in which they may dig, little swings which they can use themselves, small seesaws, blocks, or boards to build with—all these are ways in which small children can play even though they have no guidance.

We have thus to deal with two exactly opposite needs. We need the playground with its play leader and apparatus, to concentrate the play of the older children of the neighborhood; and we need play facilities at frequent intervals, over a large area, for the babies and little children, so that they may be separated into small groups and may play without other leadership than that of the older children or adults who may accompany them.

In America we have not as yet clearly differentiated between these two needs. Not one of our parks is so equipped as to afford this special opportunity for the play of small children, and no play equipment is provided near the homes.

The latter need is well illustrated on Riverside Drive in New York City, where an open parking approximately one mile long and thirty feet wide affords play space for thousands of little children every day. It would be unwise to have these very small children brought together in a playground. A wise provision would be to place a sand pile every hundred yards or so, each of which would attract a small number of babies. The idea is to have a large number of small groups, in contrast to the playground idea, which is to have a small number of large groups.

In Berlin this plan has already been carried out. Down the middle of some of the broader avenues there are walks and trees; and here, every few days, loads of clean sand are placed short distances apart. In each sand pile a few children can be found playing happily under the supervision of their mothers, nurses, or older brothers and sisters. These sand piles need not be unsightly, nor do they need to destroy the beauty of the boulevard. Small circular basins, having brick floors and a rounded concrete coping, could be embedded in the turf, making attractive centres for the little groups.

In the ordinary playground it has been found necessary to reserve a certain part of the ground exclusively for the little children, placing them in charge of a kindergartner or some person with similar training. Would it not be wise,

SEPARATION VS. CONCENTRATION

wherever possible, to have these small equipments distributed throughout a city, close to the homes of the small children, rather than to attempt to bring the babies together in large numbers on the playgrounds?

CHAPTER III

HUNTING AND FIGHTING PLAYS

ONE of the vivid impressions of my early fatherhood was seeing one of my own children, aged four, chasing another, aged six. The older child was running for the piazza of the house, and, before reaching it, I saw her and was arrested by the expression of fear on her face. The pupils of her eyes were dilated, her nostrils were playing as they do in extreme fear, her face was white and her breath drawn. They were playing bear, and the smaller girl was the bear. There was no danger that the "bear" would catch her; she could run faster than her sister. She had never been told bear stories which might have accounted for her fright. Yet this fear had come from somewhere and laid hold of her. I stopped her and counted her heart; it was beating 130. This illustrates a set of feelings all children have, though not often so intensely.

Almost every one has recollections of this kind. There is my own remembrance of playing "black man" when I was eight. The two

HUNTING AND FIGHTING PLAYS 17

sides of the street serve as goals in this game, and one person in the middle is "it." The object of the game is to run from one side to the other without being tagged. I remember running until it seemed to me I could not stand up; I could not possibly have run faster. It was all for fear that if I were caught I would be "it." And what then would have happened? Nothing; I would simply be "it." The fear of this amounted to panic. I also remember running for "home" in hide-and-seek, just at dusk, when it seemed as though something might jump from behind a bush or tree, tearing for "home" with my pursuer keeping an unchanging distance behind and my heart racing because of the fear. I have crouched behind door or bush, waiting for the one who was "seeking" me, with my heart thumping so I thought he would surely hear. All this is true of many children in playing hide-and-seek. Even when they are quite still, the heart will run up to over 100. Nothing is going to happen, but this old, old fear, the fear of being caught, has possession of them.

And when a child is "it," and does not know whether he can catch the other person or reach the goal first, he will run until the world swims in front of him. He must catch the other; it is necessary, he will stop at nothing, taking dangerous chances. It is a perfectly unreasonable feeling. There is no cause for fear, no reason for the heart to run up to 100 or 130 when he is behind a bush and the pursuing person passes by. There is nothing in what the child is doing which bears any relation to any experience in his past life, nor in his father's, his grandfather's, as far as he can know. Yet this feeling of terror in being caught is common to all mankind.

When my boy was less than two years old I would start toward him as if I were going to catch him. I had never been rough with him, but he would scream and run across the room and hide his face. Then when I sat down he would want me to do it again. There was no reason for him to scream and run away so desperately; he knew I was not going to hurt him. He had seen no one else run away; he was not mimicking. He had had no experience either with me or with any one else to cause that feeling. Yet whenever I started toward him, away he would go. He was in the power of this same instinct feeling.

My wife told me when she was nine years old she was playing tag with some children in the school yard. A boy chased her; she raced around the yard, up the stairs, into the classroom, and

HUNTING AND FIGHTING PLAYS 19

hid under the teacher's desk. She must not be caught; it would never do to get caught. She had that same feeling.

Records of plays based on the fear of being caught and the exaltation in catching, secured from many parts of the world, show that they are found everywhere. The Chinese feelings are like ours, the Hawaiian feelings are like ours, expressed in the same way. We are quite safe, with the evidence we have, in saying that this is a world-wide experience which grips, not every individual, but certainly nine out of ten of all who play tag during childhood. They have all been seized by the feeling of exaltation, on the one hand, and the sense of fear on the other. These two desires—to catch and to escape being caught—are sufficiently strong to call forth every bit of human power in running and skill in dodging. These motives are dominant throughout life, merely attaching themselves to other activities—the escaping of penalty, the pursuing of the thing desired, the exaltation in its attainment. The feelings themselves arise and come to power in most of us through playing some form of tag. Ultimately they can be turned into other paths, and used in other ways, but the tag play affords one of the earliest and most common ways for their development.

These early hunting feelings are not merely mimic feelings, imitating real desires of a later age; they are themselves real. The little girl who ran away from the bear was not imagining a fear; she was in a panic which had physiological effects. An imitation fear could not dilate the pupils and cause the heart to beat as hers did. The desire to catch, to hunt, is a desire which has very real results in action. A group of boys of about fourteen years of age in passing through the woods saw a little snake. There was no reason for killing that snake, and the boys were not inherently cruel, yet, by this almost universal feeling, the snake was promptly despatched. If the masculine individual is turned loose where there is anything to kill, he wants to kill it. Not only boys, but men, good men, educated men, do that and enjoy it. When such men as President Roosevelt want to rest they go out into the woods and hunt, satisfying their consciences by collecting, or other excuses.

I have recorded for a year, as far as I could, through Spalding's and other firms that sell sporting goods, the amount of money spent on game preserves. In one year we spent over $10,000,000 to hunt and kill things which we did not need to eat. In that same year there were 48 men killed in the Maine woods alone.

HUNTING AND FIGHTING PLAYS

I knew of a man who killed 287 ducks in one day. On a cold, early winter morning he sat still for hours, in an uncomfortable position, getting things for which he had no need. From a calm, intellectual view-point it was a very stupid performance. But there was this old instinctive basis of desire which justified the man in his own sight.

Closely connected with the hunting interest is the interest in a fight. I met a Columbia professor who has charge of one of the branches of æsthetics, and is a mild, gentle man, courteous and of a fine nature. He was much elated over having seen two longshoremen fighting on South Street, which borders on the East River. He said there was a large crowd and that the men were evenly matched. I asked: "What did you do? Call a policeman?" "No," he answered, then added: "It was a perfectly fair fight, nothing wrong about it." He had not seen anything for months that pleased him more. He explained that all modern life is so indirect; we smile and are polite; we do nothing straight out. His feeling was the old masculine interest in a fight asserting itself.

All over the world, in all stages of civilization, very large proportions of men have been interested in all kinds of fighting. In China they have trained crickets and men come together to make their crickets fight. Wherever there are cocks there are game fights, with men watching and wagering about the results. In Spain there is the public bull-fight. In all Anglo-Saxon countries there is boxing, which still continues in spite of legislation. Frequently those agencies which handle the world's news give more space to a discussion whether one man of a certain weight will succeed in knocking out another man in a given number of rounds, than they give to an election. This is a most peculiar phenomenon, if one forgets the history of mankind, and simply looks at the immediate present interest, aside from any utility, which man has in fighting.

The two great topics of literature are love and fighting. Practically all the fiction in the world is built upon a combination of these two interests. If we took love out of all the stories, we should still have a choice collection; if we took fighting out, there would still remain a large number of books; but if we took out both love and fighting, the world's poetry, romance, art, and literature would be gone, for these two are the basic human emotions, and our understanding of the world's history would be gone. Hence when boys in their teens read dime novels they

HUNTING AND FIGHTING PLAYS 23

are doing what the rest of the world has always done. When they read books which convey impressions false to life, in which the fighting instinct is perverted, it is bad for them. But fighting of some kind is part of character; it is no superficial, modern thing.

Under modern conditions there is no real use for the kind of fighting which most of us still persist in having. Yet it still fascinates us. The interest shown in the naval battles and the war between Russia and Japan was not purely an interest in the triumph of righteousness; it was a great fight. Victory for the Japanese advanced them further in the world's estimation and respect than centuries of commercial or industrial success would have done. The combat against tuberculosis is a far more deadly fight than any war in the world, more full of danger and suffering to the families of our nation. But it is not dramatic. Hence more money and time and interest are given in connection with any great pugilistic fight than for so non-exciting a thing as the combat against tuberculosis.

A desire to throw hard and straight is part of the fighting interest. Doctor Raycroft, of the University of Chicago, gives this account of his feelings in playing golf. Sometimes he made two or three good drives, hitting the ball far and hard. After that he had a satisfied feeling for many days, a kind of satisfaction his work never gave. He used to play on a baseball team; he says that a hard throw which went straight and accomplished its aim gave a kind of pleasure that was organic. Other men feel this same interest in throwing. I was walking one day on a beach with four or five companions, all of them doctors of medicine, philosophy, or law. We were discussing some question concerning Hegel's philosophy, when I saw an empty bottle on the beach. I remarked to myself: "I will try the relative attractiveness of Hegel's philosophy and this desire to throw." I took the bottle, tossed it about twenty paces into the water, and picked up stones to throw at it. Every man followed my example; every man wanted to break that bottle. These men were not unique; men and boys who play ball belong to all peoples.

Facts of this kind seem to point to one conclusion. Mere fondness for exercise does not account for this interest. I once tried to produce games constructed purely with reference to using many different neuro-muscular combinations. I thought I could combine gymnastics with athletics and get the best results through the use of many movements, not merely

HUNTING AND FIGHTING PLAYS 25

running, throwing, and striking. But the children, when they were by themselves, would not play the games. There was no "go" in them. Gradually it became clear to me that the instincts back of this particular group of activities are so definite that it is impossible even to regulate the neuro-muscular co-ordinations involved. They are tremendously old instincts, older than civilized history, older than savage history.

A great many years ago, probably in the early part of the Pleistocene age, before there were any records such as we have now of man as man, before he had invented or obtained fire or learned its use, before he had developed weapons, before he had learned to build houses and structures, when he still lived in caves or in rude platforms in trees, there existed with him the great animals of the world, which have since been killed or subdued. The sabre-toothed tiger, the great sloth were still alive, and some of the great lizards. Here was man; he had no jaws that could bite as animals bite; he had no talons that could hold and kill as could the talons of the great fighting animals; he had no claws like the members of the cat family; he had no thick skin like the rhinoceros, or the shell of the turtle; he had no speed, such as had the deer or the dog or the horse. In all these respects he was suited only to be food for the great flesh-eating animals.

During this time running was of importance to man. He who could run the fastest and longest was the best-equipped for getting food and also for escaping in moments of danger. So there was a constant elimination of the non-runners and a constant survival of the runners. The boys who liked to run, who had instinctive desires for running, survived and grew into men. It followed that there was a development in boyhood of this desire to run, this interest in hiding and dodging, out of which gradually grew these tag games, which antedate written history. They antedate even the rude records written on the walls of the cave-dwellers. They go back to animal time, these games of tag, and are merely the elaboration of the hunted and hunting feelings which all the survivors possessed.

Presently, as man developed, he found that to take the limb of a tree and strip it of its branches gave him a power the animals did not have. He could stand behind cover and strike. The use of the club lengthened his arm and gave weight and power. The man who learned to handle this tree limb quickly, with strength and skill, was far better able to survive and get food

HUNTING AND FIGHTING PLAYS 27

for his family than the man who failed to develop this ability. A third impulse developed with these two—the desire to throw. There is something still more effective than the ability to use a club. A stone, half the size of the fist, can be thrown for fifty yards with sufficient accuracy and power to break the leg of a deer, and cripple or kill a smaller animal. It was an effective weapon in defending the home. So this ability to throw hard and straight became one of the great things in the world of boys; those who liked it best and practised it most became the men who survived. The stone was the first weapon that could strike from a distance; it thus served to eliminate differences in size and strength. No animal had a weapon of this kind. Certain fish can project a drop of water and catch a fly, and there are certain apes that throw cocoanuts from a height; but to stand on a level and throw straight and hard is distinctively human. This ability to throw, this love of throwing, is one of the things that through thousands of years has grown deep down into our natures, and is still of fundamental interest.

From the use of the club and the throwing of stones man has developed the fighting and defensive implements. He made the boomerang, which is a flat club curved; the spear, a straight club with a sharp end; the arrow, a little spear to throw from the end of a string. From the bow and arrow developed the crossbow, of which the modern rifle is the descendant. The great Roman catapult for throwing heavy weights came from the same sources. Man was then more able to compete with the early animals, but the love of running and throwing and striking still survived, for these were still the fundamental co-ordinations underlying his new weapons. So the children of the men who liked to do these things had an especially good chance of growing up, and they in turn liked to play games that involved running, throwing, and striking. Those are the athletics of the world to-day. This, I believe, is the natural history of athletic sports.

Examining all the tag games we find running and dodging; in baseball, running and striking; lacrosse, running, dodging, catching, throwing with an implement; polo, running on horseback, striking; basket-ball, running, throwing, catching. They are all built with an emphasis on one or the other of these three activities. Billiards are different; solitaire is different; but the great athletic games are based on the fundamental activities that have been cited.

HUNTING AND FIGHTING PLAYS

Fighting plays may be divided into two groups—direct and indirect fighting plays. Direct fighting plays accomplish defeat by giving injury. Included in these plays are:

    Boxing   Fencing
    Wrestling   Football.

In boxing defeat consists in being unable to go on; in wrestling, victory belongs to him who can put his adversary's hips and shoulders on the mat. In the indirect fighting plays victory inheres in more objective and external results, consisting perhaps of a score, or a number of points. All games of competition may be classed as indirect fighting plays, when the degree of competition is sufficiently strong so as to predominate over other elements in the play. The despair and emulation in a competitive game correspond to the same emotions in a fight.

This raises the question of the extent to which we should encourage fighting games. The fact that these activities were once useful does not in itself prove that they are so still. Man no longer relies for his life's safety on the ability to throw hard and straight. He has conquered the great animals of the world, and his future career does not depend on the extermination of the few remaining large, dangerous beasts. The present significance of athletic sports, however, does not lie in their relation to muscular strength and skill. It lies in their relation to moral qualities. Courage was developed in man through the necessity of facing difficult and dangerous situations, through fighting, and fighting desperately, when the odds were against him. The means used were running, throwing, and striking; these were the co-ordinations which became connected with courage. The disregard of pain came into being through standing and fighting regardless of suffering. Those agencies which shaped the neuro-muscular co-ordinations of the human arm no less truly shaped the fundamental qualities of manhood which we regard as necessary to moral life—courage, endurance, the willingness to hang on and finish when one is sorely punished. All the active and positive virtues are related to these old activities.

There is, of course, no real connection between muscular movement and courage; but when man has had to use his courage for thousands of years in ways involving certain muscular co-ordinations, the two have come to be associated. When we desire to cultivate courage in a boy we do not read him maxims concerning the beauty of courage. We put him in situations that correspond to the old situations in which his forebears had to develop courage or

HUNTING AND FIGHTING PLAYS 31

go under. These situations we find now in the form of play, and, in this form, the boy can have the education without the physical danger. The attitude of the boy who can play a vigorous, hard-fought game and control his temper—who can run on and finish the race, no matter how tired, no matter if his heart is pounding and objects are growing black before him—is significant, not from the standpoint of muscular development, but of moral development. The natural tendency of the boy is to win these virtues in this old way; these are the means by which courage and power came to man. We need not expect these qualities in our boys unless we give them similar opportunities, or opportunities which will act as substitutes.

Of course we cannot have real fights in large communities; the actual situations which develop the virtues of courage, endurance, scorn of pain, are no longer possible. It seems more necessary now than ever to get what development can be secured in connection with plays involving these old activities. It is still necessary for man to be courageous, but courageous in a different way. It is necessary for him to be a fighter, but not in the sense of killing. The courage that keeps a man straight and clean in politics is a far more difficult form of courage than that called forth in the old days. But, in the main, it comes in the same way. There is no way of creating courage; it must be developed. All that we can do is to create opportunity for its exercise.

When boys have no chance to play games of the hunting and fighting type, they have little opportunity to develop those qualities that make fighters of men, and there is as much need of fighters as there ever was. If temptations were ever strong they are strong in our modern cities. Safeguards have been let down and modern life has been made lax to an extent that it has never been before in the history of the world, as regards high moral and physical standards. We are protected from cold, we have food, clothing, and shelter; immediate physical danger and suffering have been practically eliminated. It seems as if the effect of modern life is to produce ease, mushiness, softness, and when grave dangers arise there has been developed no strength with which to grapple them. Hence here is the need of boxing, of football, of games that teach the despising of pain and danger, for these qualities are related to power and the tissue of character. If ever there was need of a stiff-backed boy, it is in the modern city.

CHAPTER IV

PLAYING HOUSE

NEARLY all children have at some time or other played house. At the age of four I was given an umbrella, which I set up on my bed. I found a shawl and some pins and draped the shawl over the umbrella so as to make a little house to sit in. I said to myself, "This is *my* house." The feeling associated with that statement can never be explained to a person who has not had it. I had the same feeling—very comfortable and deep—when, after being married, we moved into two small rooms in a boarding-house in New York; that was our house.

My own experience as a boy is often brought to mind when on travelling through the woods I see the little shelters that boys build, a tree house, a cave, a wigwam of green stems or small trees. These habitations are often made by boys who have good homes, who are not in need of seeking shelter; these dwellings are made for no reason which the boys themselves can give. Frequently a part of the floor is dug up, and stores of chestnuts are collected underneath. In none of the playhouses I ever had could we stand up straight. There was a little raised platform in the middle on which we made a fire, and we sat in very uncomfortable positions. We were too hot in front and too cold in the back. The smoke filled our eyes. Meanwhile we were eating partly baked potatoes or half-burned chestnuts or doughnuts taken from mother's pantry; and we had feelings of comfort, of being at home, such as we never experienced in school or in our parents' dwellings. We recognize these feelings later in life when we come to establish our own homes, and have our own kitchens and tables and hearth-fires. These states of mind are not dependent on reason; they are made up of profound instinct feelings. The feelings which centred in one of these shanties were sufficiently strong to tie a group of boys together. We would fight with a neighboring group and steal their stores if we could. We were protecting our own home, our own people.

These feelings are common to most children, and are experienced by girls and boys alike, although the girl's shelter feelings seem to differ somewhat from those of boys. Many of my friends have furnished incidents from their own experiences.

PLAYING HOUSE

"In our nursery stood an old-fashioned three-quarter bed," says one, "with sides to keep the little ones from falling out. The four legs continued up into posts which supported a mosquito bar. This bed made a house with two stories, one under the bed, the other within the railed enclosure with a shawl to serve as a protecting roof. It is useless to try to describe our feeling of protection when enclosed in this comfortable dwelling. A chair served as steps to the upper story, and one child lived down-stairs while the others occupied the floor above. We made constant visitations up and down."

A corner of the dining-room screened by high clothes-bars covered with shawls served as the first "house" for another friend. Still another records a large variety of houses. A great oak-tree formed one of these. Tents made of bed-sheets with an umbrella for centre-pole were used for evening and morning play. "We also made houses by sweeping up sand into little walls three inches high. Higher mounds of sand were used for seats, and a pile of bricks formed the stove. These houses were many-roomed, and it was forbidden to cross over the sand walls, except at certain spots where we had made doors. At times, however, we preferred smaller houses which we could occupy entirely alone, screened even from the sight of passers-by."

Small indoor houses seem to belong especially to the experience of younger children, and the house plays increase in complexity as children grow older.

Another friend used to make a tent out of the bedposts and sheets. A strong sheet was stretched from post to post and tied, and the sides of the "house" were draped with bedding, to keep out the enemy—in some cases imaginary, in other cases the smaller sisters. This form of house play continued for a long time, and had many variations and additions. At first the tent was used as a home, and the interior was separated into rooms by rows of pillows. Sometimes the space below the bed was a cellar or a cave filled with wild animals. Later the children made use of a heavy down comforter with which they built a cave. The party then divided into cave-dwellers and cliff-dwellers, sometimes visiting each other, sometimes waging war for the possession of each other's dwellings.

The same friend who writes of these experiences moved at the age of eleven to a house surrounded by many acres of land. A large apple-tree, with low-hanging branches, was

PLAYING HOUSE

adapted to the needs of a playhouse. Boards were nailed from limb to limb, and the house was divided into many rooms. This much more complicated arrangement suited the demands of older children.

Sometimes, in wanderings from the home-tree, the children played at being lost in the orchard, and as imaginary night came on, they found it necessary to hunt a suitable place for shelter from storm and wild animals. On the top of a hill, behind the house, was a group of pines, dark and cool, and "different" from the rest of the orchard. Under these pines they always made a temporary shelter, protected from the terrors of the dark by a packing-box and a fire. Foraging parties went out for food, cautiously entering the cellar and stealing potatoes from the bin. And out in that box, on a sweltering day, the children crouched before a hot fire, eating smoky, half-raw potatoes (they could never be prevailed upon to eat potatoes at the table), and were supremely happy. They had been lost, but had made a shelter for themselves. They felt protected and at home.

Another friend's playhouse experience always took the form of a wigwam, usually inhabited with some companion. They built wigwams of clothes and quilts, and later of willow sticks tied together. These formed a defense which other boys tried to tear down. A great feeling of mystery was always connected with these structures. They had to be concealed. In a copse twenty-five or thirty feet above the travelled road the boys sat with a shawl and plaited the branches together to make the place more hidden. It was a great joy to make a horrible noise to terrify the countrymen going by, but the boys felt as terrified as those who passed.

Even the crowded conditions under which city children live have not deprived them of this desire to find a place of their own, where they can feel at home, protected, sheltered. One of the common things for children to do in a city back yard is to get chunks of coal, or blocks of wood, or even a nail, and mark divisions in the earth. One sees these markings, also, on the asphalt pavement of the sidewalks. "This is my house. This is your house." And it feels different when they are in "my" house from what it does when they are in "your" house. As far as I observed, the feelings of the house play are stronger with girls than with boys.

Boys are especially interested in the construction of houses. A gang of boys in a district school in central New York built a house in a fence corner. All the boys of the neighborhood were invited to join in the enterprise, but as soon as the work actually began the group became a closed corporation. This is a most significant fact in its bearing on the connection of the shelter feeling to group life. No boy who had refused to assist was afterward allowed to come into the house. The walls were built of flat stones, piled as high as the top of the fence. Short rails served as rafters, and the whole was well covered with brush. One of the boys was chosen leader; his word thereafter became absolute law. That organization was the beginning of a "gang." The boys hurried from school in the afternoon and used every available minute for the completion of the house. Then cooking experiments were tried over a fire that never cooked anything, but burned and scorched and blackened, filling the house with smoke that refused to go up the hole prepared for it.

The friend who tells of this stone house adds: "My feeling of intense personal ownership was never duplicated until about four years ago, when my wife and I purchased a house and established a home for the first time. Two years ago I happened to pass the spot where the old rail fence once stood. Not a trace of the playhouse remained, but upon gazing at the site the same thrill came over me that I used to feel as I squeezed through the narrow door and sat on those torturous seats, with a sharp stone or a jagged rail digging a hole in my back. I have never found an upholstered chair that could compare with those seats for comfort, and that could give in equal measure the sense of being at home."

If we look back over the history of the human race, and consider what shelter has meant to us and how civilization would have been impossible without this development of the interest in the "house," we begin to see the survival value which these feelings, now expressed in the play of children, have had for our kind. Those individuals who had the inclination to remain in one place, rather than to wander, had a great advantage over the rest. Remaining in one place would result inevitably in greater accumulation of property, and out of property much of our social custom and law have grown. The massing together of pottery, baskets, religious properties, cooking utensils, ornaments, changes of clothing, with all that this accumulation means for the advance of civilization, is greatly facilitated by remaining in one place. Those people who had the feeling for shelter gradually obtained these advantages.

The establishment of the home in one place,

with comparatively little wandering, was also favorable to the growth of small children. In the home there was less danger from exposure. There was less danger from enemies, since accurate knowledge of the immediate physical environment was a great help in any combat. The domestication of plants and animals can be carried out only by residence, for a time at least, in one locality. Such domestication means increasing freedom from the daily pressure for food. It means an opportunity of growth for the higher mental life; it means increasing stability of the home and the social group.

Of course, one could not maintain that the early races adopted shelter because they perceived that it would be advantageous and that through it all these blessings would accrue to them. They had no such conscious purpose. But it is nevertheless true that the individuals and groups in whom the feeling for locality and shelter was most strongly developed inevitably gained these benefits. Their children had a better chance of survival. So the shelter feeling was passed on and strengthened among the civilized peoples, for it was one of the factors that made those peoples.

There seems to be a difference on the part of various races with regard to the shelter feeling.

Out of the lower East Side in New York 40,000 people migrated in a short time across the Williamsburg Bridge and settled in what is known as Brownsville. There was plenty of room in Brownsville. There were many vacant lots. But the people packed together as tightly in Brownsville as they had been on the lower East Side. They had not this feeling for individual shelter.

It seems that in the Aryan invasion of Europe the people in the different waves of the invasion possessed different feelings with reference to the home. The first comers, the Northmen, demanded individual shelter. Every man wanted his own roof, alone; when the young people married they set up a separate establishment. That feeling has remained until the present time, and those of us who are of Norman stock object much more strenuously to the tenement house and the apartment than do people of some other races.

When the young people of the Southern nations married they simply put on an addition to the old dwelling, which became larger as the family grew. The people went to their farms during the day, sometimes at great distances and in many directions, but they all returned to the central place at night. That is, their feeling for family unity and group life differed from that of the Northern peoples. Both these feelings, however, are based on the feeling for shelter.

The present conditions of city life are affecting to some extent this desire for a particular locality and a particular shelter. All the movement of the times is away from continuous living in one place. From the kindergarten up things belong in common. The house is a temporary home. People in Boston move on an average once a year; other cities are probably much the same in this respect. We are very far removed from the feeling for locality which some Hawaii Islanders had of whom I have heard. They had left a small island on which nothing grew but a few palm-trees. They had come away in a group, so that the element of the loss of friends entered into the situation but slightly. But they grew so desperately homesick that some of them died. They wanted *their place*. A feeling of this kind does not survive in the modern city.

Continuity of character tends to grow out of attachment to a place. One of the most dangerous factors in city life is this ease of moving. A person may leave readily the scene of his actions for another part of the town, and the modern makeshift known as a "bluff" may be developed in place of character. The sense of responsibility for past deeds is weakened when a man no longer faces their consequences in the locality where they were committed. Constant moving tends to loss of the feeling for home, and all that this feeling implies for group life and mutual responsibility.

There is great need for encouraging this feeling for shelter and home through the plays of children. It may also be encouraged in other ways. My own children went back every summer to the locality where we had lived for sixteen years. They knew the people and the people knew us. The children knew where crabs were to be found, where clams abounded, and where they could fish for trout. They had associations with various places. There was the spot where one of them fell, there the place where we first raised the flag. That means continuity. During the winter they lived in Springfield, in New York, in Boston, and went to different schools. New ties were constantly made and constantly broken. This easy change makes for superficiality of character, unless it is balanced by some sort of continuity. One of the things which we must give our children is opportunity to develop their feelings for shelter and home by attachment to some locality, and by

PLAYING HOUSE 45

the various activities which come under the head of "playing house."

This is true, also, with regard to the other play so frequently connected with playing house —the preparation and eating of food. One of the interesting things that small children do is to make mud pies. Sometimes mud pies have really been tasted, in an attempt to carry the play to an extreme conclusion. When the children grow older, they frequently progress to real cookery of a more or less primitive type, often carried on in connection with the plays of shelter. Boys are as much interested in their way in the mimic preparation of food as girls are. I have already mentioned the doughnuts and half-baked potatoes eaten in the shanty which I had with some other boys in the woods. We also used to kill and cook English sparrows. I ate those meals with an enthusiasm which I have never known in eating anything else in my life. It was a great joy to make little loaves of bread and cake, and to have stores where we sold food. In connection with a house that my children built, they had a complete set of cooking utensils. There was nothing cooked on the real stove in the real house that was not also cooked on the little stove in the playhouse.

A very real sense of increased power comes to

the individual who is efficient in these activities of the home. There are feelings of complacency, enlarged personality, independence. There is a great difference between our feeling toward food that we have prepared ourselves or that some one at home has prepared for us, and our feeling toward hotel food.

Two great factors have always held the family together—shelter and food. The kitchen has been the social centre of the family during all time. Eating and the preparation of food have been connected with the development of social life. The kitchen with the copper pots on the wall was the place to which the neighbors would come, and the fact that we now set apart a separate room for the reception of visitors is socially an abnormal procedure. When people know each other well, they go out into the kitchen together.

When people eat together they have expressed a definite social relation. They feel differently about each other. Frequently, if a man wants to ask a favor of another, he invites him to dinner; in that way he establishes a new relation. This set of feelings is one against which many intellectual people rebel. When the effort is made to get them together and it is suggested that they have something to eat, they say that

PLAYING HOUSE

you want to put something into their stomachs. This statement is not wholly true. "Putting something into one's stomach" does not express it. The symbol of breaking bread and eating salt together is a truer one. The common meal is the sign of fellowship. The cooking of food tends to bring people together. It is a basal element in the evolution of the social life. The meal is the time when men are free to meet. Hence the social activities grow up naturally at a meal, and the social traditions are associated with the partaking of salt and the breaking of bread. The state of the body after eating is favorable to social life. There is quiet and rest rather than hostility. A fundamental desire has been gratified. Hence the establishment of friendly relations is easy.

The cooking of food has in the past contributed to racial advance and survival. Cooking means a great increase in the quantity of the available food-supply. It enables men to dry and preserve meats. It provides foods which could not be eaten uncooked. It aids the digestion of food. For all these reasons it tends toward greater vigor, and hence toward survival.

Therefore, the playing with food seems to be another of the important preparations for life, because it gives the child an opportunity to express and so develop the instinctive feelings in connection with which so much of our racial growth has come about.

CHAPTER V
FIRE PLAY

BEHIND our house in Springfield, Massachusetts, was a sand waste, with a bank of sand four feet high. The face of the bank had been dug away so that it could be burrowed into. Periodically the interests of our children would centre about this bank; it was an ideal place for fire play. The children built their fires at various places in the bank. They would burrow a hole some feet from the top of the bank and make an upward excavation to serve as a chimney. Viewed from above, the bank presented a flat surface riddled with chimney holes.

Playing with fire is a little dangerous, and yet children cannot come to know fire except by playing with it in the same way as they have learned to know other things through play. Hence, while fire play was encouraged in our home, it was restricted to one day a week. Friday was always fire day, when the children were allowed to have as many fires as they wished, and fires of every kind. They wore woollen dresses as a precaution, and some older person was always present. In the main the children preferred small fires with which they could do things to large fires which were merely spectacular. If a fire could be made to cook something it was enjoyed particularly.

Ownership in these little fires was passionate and intense. One of my girls ran to me once in great excitement, saying: "Father, Louise put a stick on my fire and I didn't say she could." That fire was her own; it was tied up with her self as much as any other possession that she had. The care with which the children attended to their individual fires, the selection of suitable material, was a matter of all-absorbing interest. There was great anxiety lest the fire should go out, not because it was needed, but simply because it was wanted. It could be lit again from another fire, but that was not satisfactory to the child; one's own fire must be kept going.

The feelings that children have toward fire vary with the size of the fire. There are feelings of tenderness for a small fire, of sympathy and anxiety lest it should die. There are feelings of fear toward a big blaze, even if there be no danger from it. It appears that girls' feelings dif-

FIRE PLAY 51

fer on the whole from boys', the girl inclining toward the little, domesticated fire, and the boy toward the large, fierce, dramatic blaze. There are feelings of excitement in connection with a roaring fire and of revery with a dying glow. Of all these feelings I have numerous records, and probably all of us have such records, if not written, then recorded in brain cells and visual images.

These feelings about fire are by no means confined to children. In our home we had a fair-sized fireplace, in which three-foot logs could be placed. The room in which the fireplace was located held from thirty to forty persons. I have repeatedly tried the experiment of having the logs ready to light, so as to avoid all preliminary and disturbing work which might distract the attention, and then when the room was full of friends, chattering as friends always do, lighting the fire. An open fire was not so uncommon a sight as to awaken any feeling of the unusual, for we had it practically every day, but its effect was almost always profound. With the lighting of the fire came first a lowering of the conversational tone, then a lessening in its quantity, and frequently a full stop. I have timed many pauses of over thirty seconds' duration, and one of forty-three seconds. On the latter occasion over twenty persons were present in the room, and there was no single psychological cause for the stopping of conversation. Psychologists who have studied the behavior of groups of people know that ordinarily no cause of an internal character is likely to arise which will stop the talk of twenty people simultaneously. A half-minute's pause in a prayer-meeting seems interminable, painful; but before the fire it is different; one feels only reverence and awe.

The effect of fire in producing a sense of protection is even to-day experienced frequently. Late one afternoon two boys and I were lost in the Adirondack woods. We tramped about until night came on, and there was no hope of finding our way. We walked in total darkness; there was no difference between looking up and looking down in the woods. We smashed into tree trunks and could not distinguish between the trees and the sky. It was raining hard, our blankets were wet, and we had little to eat. We found a brook by the sound of its rippling; near it we discovered a dry, hollow oak log, and with our last few matches we made a fire.

The state of feeling before we built that fire had been one of unreasoning despair. We were not in a dangerous situation, for that part of the country is thickly settled. There was no probability of our starving to death. But the awfulness of being lost, of being out of touch with human beings, not knowing where we were, and our friends not knowing where we were—these feelings were so intense as to blind the reason, not only of the boys, but of myself. The situation seemed desperate. With the lighting of the fire our state of feeling changed to one of comfort and satisfaction. The actual conditions were the same as before. We were as much lost as we had been. We were no farther from nor any nearer to other people. There was no special danger from which we were protected by the fire. It was raining so hard that the fire did not even change our physical comfort in any striking manner. But our whole attitude toward life became different. The place of the fire acquired the significance of home. We sat up most of the night feeding the flame, and when we went off to get wood and returned to the fire we felt that we were no longer lost.

Lying down by a large fire at night in the woods never fails to produce in me feelings of safety and the comfort of being at home. A party of which I was one tramped seven weeks through the Yosemite Valley. The camp fire was the centre about which we would gather. As soon as it was lit at night, we had a feeling of unity. If we went away for some hours to draw water, or to get a better grazing ground for the horses, going back to the fire was "going home." That was the phrase we used. If we returned to a place after having been absent for some time, we invariably had the fire in the same spot in which we had built it before. Some years ago I experimented with this feeling by deliberately keeping away from a known camp fire. I found that I had a sense of uneasiness, of wanting to get there. Going into the woods and having for company only the birds and the plants is not sufficient; but a fire goes a long way to supply the need of companionship. It feels as if it were alive; it gives the sense of home.

Ascending smoke produces feelings of an æsthetic nature in many people. A striking fireplace which I once saw in California made its appeal in this way. The fire was built on the stone floor against a wall, flanked by two large posts; the chimney hole in the ceiling was placed slightly forward for the sake of the draught. The fire and smoke rose in an unbroken column against the wall from floor to ceiling. It was a sight which one could watch

FIRE PLAY 55

hour after hour, spellbound by the combined effect of smoke and flame.

There is fascination about the smoke from a large fire on which green wood or green pine-needles have been piled. When there is no wind, a solid, gray, fluted column, perhaps a foot in diameter, goes up motionless for two or three feet, and than breaks into rhythmical waves. The smoke motion has something almost hypnotic. There is a similar feeling about the thin gray line of smoke ascending from incense, and gradually spreading out into nothingness. To get the best effect, sticks of Chinese incense must be placed in a room in which every door and window has been closed, on a day when there is little wind. The columns will go up without a break for a long way, passing finally into beautiful gray whirls and rings.

It is said that blind people do not care to smoke. Smoking in the dark is exceedingly unsatisfactory. If one is not really attentive to a pipe, it will go out unawares. I have been told by a friend that he knows of few things more annoying than to be smoking away on a pipe and suddenly discovering that it has been out for some time. It is the visual sense to a large degree that sets up these smoke reactions. One of the charms of smoking is the vision of gray whirls, streams, clouds, rings of impalpable smoke, ever changing their form, ever suggesting, never realizing. They grip one's imagination.

People behold visions on looking into a fire, particularly a fire with embers. Many stories are built on what one sees at such times. We can have a sullen fire, a cheerful fire, an angry fire. These emotional experiences connected with fires have been well caught by Ik Marvel in his *Reveries of a Bachelor*. The portraiture of his state of feeling, of sitting and seeing the fire burn, of watching it die away, lends significance and emotion to the events related in the book. Such books are read because they are true; these are common feelings that all people have in connection with such fires.

But there are also feelings of terror connected with fire. One day the apron of our oldest daughter caught fire. From an upper window her mother saw her running to the house with the front of the apron ablaze. She hurried down-stairs and met the child at the door; but, as does not usually happen, the running had put out the fire instead of fanning it. The mother was sick for several days after that and did not recover for several weeks from a pain in the lower part of the back. Many people

FIRE PLAY

have had similar experiences. It may be, of course, that there is no special kind of fear connected with fire, and that the feeling is merely part of a general great fear; but there seems to be an abject terror aroused by fire which is not experienced in connection with other dangers, such as danger from water or wind. The heroes of youth in our cities are not those who endanger their lives for the sake of society, but the firemen who fight the flames.

I stood on the bluff in Yokohama watching one of the great fires in Tokio, twenty miles away. It was a fire three miles long, in the heart of the city. The sight of that long line of smoke twenty miles across the country excited the most intense feelings of awe and terror. Imagination flew to the scene of the fire; we knew what must be happening there. At another time I have seen a solid square of houses, equal to about eight of our city blocks, burning in Yokohama. A section of the fire was immediately opposite our own house. People who were unfamiliar with the fire fear behaved in an extraordinarily panic-stricken way. Our own house was comparatively safe, but to stand on the veranda and look at this great fire, wholly beyond the power of the Japanese engines, produced a feeling of unreasoning terror.

58   A PHILOSOPHY OF PLAY

Fire lends a mysterious effect to the telling of ghost stories. The heart beats unevenly, and the salivary glands are often affected. At Pratt High School in Brooklyn one evening an entertainment was held at which a ghost story was told. It was a very good story, but the effect on the audience was slight. Then all lights were put out and another story was told. Some alcohol mixed in salt was burned in a bowl. The man who told the second story held the bowl between his knees, and his strong features were illumined by the yellow light flashing and going. The effect upon all the listeners was very marked; one girl was carried from the room in hysterics. The story itself was no better than the first, but in the second case the great overmastering fear of the ages had been touched, the fear of the dark, the fear of the weird occasioned by flickering flame.

A group of facts such as these seems to demand some explanation which shall relate it to the development of our kind, for it seems to be evident that animals do not have the whole human range of feelings about fire. They have the elemental panic terror to an even greater degree than human beings. Cases of the rescue of horses and cattle from burning stables illustrate this. But animals do not have the desire

FIRE PLAY

to care for fire. A fire left in the woods will not be treated by animals as it is treated by man.

The whole human race has had feelings regarding the significance of fire—fire, the destroyer, and fire, the protector. Long before the earliest historical records of humankind there are evidences that our forefathers used fire. And as soon as these records begin we find the fire feelings developed perhaps as fully as we have them now—all the early care for the fire, the sacred fire in the middle of the house, the lamps which were never allowed to go out, the ceremony before the council fire, the worship of the sun. The first Greek state officers of whom we have any record were the fire-tenders. The individuals appointed to care for the fires became the later judges, magistrates, counsellors, kings.

Fire has been the centre of the family and the social life among many people. About the common fire there developed the common interests. Fire has been closely connected with the religious life of the race. Among the Aryan peoples at first the father was the custodian of the fire; later this office was transferred to one of the daughters. The virgins who kept the fires of Vesta possessed powers over life and death.

The maintenance of perpetual fire in lamps has been identified with religion in the Greek and Roman churches for many generations. To-day we ally fire with religion in our incense, our candles, though not to the same extent as did the early peoples. I need only mention the fire-worshippers. In the Old Testament we hear of the worship of Moloch, and the kings who "made their sons pass through the fire" as a gift to the gods. The first quarrel mentioned in the Bible was about smoke. Cain complained that his smoke went along the ground, while Abel's ascended straight to heaven; and so Cain killed Abel. The behavior of smoke was indicative of the attitude of the Governing Power. Fire among many peoples has been the symbol of the soul, the living thing, that which subsists on matter but is not matter, that which has no body but consumes body.

The council fire was one which bore no relation itself to the process of deliberation going on around it. Yet deliberation and revery have been associated so often with the council fire and smoking together that it is difficult to think of the connection as a purely accidental one. The feeling that fire is related to all great occasions still survives in many civic celebrations. In Germany and Scandinavia the fires that are

FIRE PLAY 61

lit at Easter trace their origin to the ancient celebration at the return of the sun god, Balder. The vision of most of our American cities on election night is a vision of what the normal boy or girl does when he or she gets the opportunity. Fires are on the streets of the large cities by the thousands; the children have made preparations for them weeks in advance. The policemen have their minds otherwise occupied at the time.

These feelings of the significance of fire, running through all human history, raise the question of its meaning in connection with the development of our kind. There must be some reason why these feelings have been preserved by natural selection—by the law that those tribes and species shall survive which have characteristics best fitting them to survive. Man alone of all living beings has learned to master fire, and this mastery has been a great force in his cultural advancement. It makes no difference whether he first took it from the overflowing, burning lava, from the stroke of lightning on some dead tree in a forest, or whether he invented it by the friction of wood against wood, by striking bamboo against bamboo—those individuals, those tribes that had the instinct feelings to care for fire were equipped for a broadening career which was not open to those who were merely afraid of fire. By learning to care for fire, those early men were able not only to escape the danger of the large, uncontrolled conflagration, but they were also able to make use of the small, controlled fire for their own convenience.

Fire was the great destroyer of the forests and towns in those days. But fire was also the best protector from animals, and animals were the chief peril of man then. His chief danger did not consist, as it did later, in plague, typhoid, smallpox, tuberculosis. He feared the sabre-toothed tiger, and the other creatures that we see in the natural-history museum. Fire served as protection from these animals. A cave with a good fire in front of it meant safety. The man of to-day, when he goes out in the forest and lies down at night beside a large, controlled fire, such as is made by piling the trunks of three or four trees together; when he covers himself with his blanket and knows that there are no other human beings within many miles, he, too, experiences those fire feelings which were of use ages ago. There may be no bears or tigers to be protected from, but he is conscious of a sense of protection. Practically all people have this feeling.

FIRE PLAY

Through fire the cold, energy-giving regions of the earth were opened up to man. Fire was the protector from cold. By means of it the food-supply could be extended. The people who controlled fire could eat foods not otherwise eatable, and they could preserve game and fruits. The forest could be cleared and fields cut out by the use of fire—a task which would otherwise have been infinitely laborious without machinery. No metals can be worked except by fire. The tribes that first cared for fire had the first use of metals and tools. All the pottery we have depends on fire. Clay baked in the sun is relatively unstable; but clay baked in the fire forms bricks which are more enduring than the granite on which rests the foundation of the earth.

For these reasons we to-day have these feelings about fire. They come from the earliest life of the human race; they are one of the great means by which the human race has survived and evolved. The sense of terror, the sense of protection, the sense of religious significance and of beauty attached to fire are part of our inheritance as human beings—a most valuable part, and closely related to our being here at all.

Fire stands essentially as the symbol of human feeling in the world.

A realization of the race value of fire, fire the domesticator, has led to the selection of the camp fire as the symbol of a great present-day social movement. "The Ode to the Fire" of the Camp Fire Girls expresses these values:

"O Fire!
　Long years ago, when our fathers fought with animals, you were their protection.
　From the cruel cold of winter, you saved them.
　When they needed food you changed the flesh of beasts into savory meat for them.
　During all the ages your mysterious flame has been a symbol to them for Spirit.
　So (to-night) we light our fire in remembrance of the Great Spirit who gave you to us."

"The Fire Maker's Desire" voices the universality and brotherhood of man associated with fire:

"As fuel is brought to the fire
So I purpose to bring
My strength,
My ambition,
My heart's desire,
My joy,
And my sorrow,
To the fire
Of humankind.

"For I will tend
As my fathers have tended,

FIRE PLAY

And my fathers' fathers
Since time began,
The fire that is called
The love of man for man,
The love of man for God."

"The Torch-Bearer's Desire" is an expression of ideals:

"That light which has been given to me,
I desire to pass undimmed to others."

So we want our children to play with fire in order that they may come fully into their racial inheritance. The child who has not had the opportunity to play with fire has missed one of the great means for the realization of mystery, in its good sense. And the person who has no consciousness of mystery fails to understand the world. If all nature seems cold, calculated science, then we have a view of the world which is certainly untrue. But that view of the whole which appreciates the relation of things, which recognizes, also, the great beyond, and knows the world not only in an intellectual but also in this feeling sense—that is an estimation which it seems to me is real. The contact of the child with the expanse of ocean, with the dark, with fire—these are among the chief ways by which the imagination reaches out, throwing its roots way down in the instinct feelings of the past, and giving the power of relationship without which life is not particularly significant. It is difficult to write poetry over a gas log.

CHAPTER VI

TOYS—CONSTRUCTION AND OWNERSHIP

AT a mother's club in a New York settlement house a discussion arose concerning what one thing each mother would like to have provided for her boys, in addition to what they already had. One thoughtful woman claimed that a wood-shed was her greatest need. "My boys have reached the age when they want to make things," she said. "They want to whittle and split and hammer; they want to build boats. But when I let them try it in our rooms, the landlord came up and very angrily declared that he would put us out if we did not stop that noise. If we only had a wood-shed where the boys could make things, I think they might grow up properly, without going on the street so much with bad boys."

This woman had noticed a common phenomenon among boys, the dawning of a desire to make things with their hands. Boys in all parts of the world have this desire. A letter from a missionary in Japan describes the number of things which two boys made in a very short time, changing in interest from one thing to another, as each was completed. For a time they busied themselves making boats—dug-outs of various shapes. Then they grew more ambitious. One of them cut a paper pattern for a tin boat, and then made it in tin and got the tinsmith to solder it together. Then they decided to make another and solder it themselves. The knowledge gained in this way was immediately applied to the repairing of an old tin lamp for a playhouse which they had built in the back yard. They also made for this house a stove out of a kerosene can. At the same time the interest in boats progressed. One of the boys made a canoe of three boards, six feet long, cut and bent into shape. It was his all-absorbing interest until he had learned to handle it perfectly on the pond. Then he abandoned it and spent a week's hard work on a canvas canoe, bending the bamboo ribs over a fire and wiring them together.

Toys with which something can be done are much more acceptable to a growing boy than toys which are completed. If he receives an engine and track all complete he is wonderfully pleased, but he does not play with it for a very long time. He exhausts its possibilities soon, and there is nothing new to be done. But if he is given the materials, ideas, and patterns for a little boat, there are hours and even days of useful play in store for him. A knife is a toy for which the average boy longs; there are so many things he can do with it. A tool of any kind, a chisel or hammer, has a similar attraction. Toys are objects in connection with which our instinct feelings have a chance to develop. They might be called pegs on the wall of the mind on which to hang instinct feelings. The doll is a peg upon which hangs the bulk of the domestic feelings of the girl. The ball and bat for the boy are toys around which are clustered and in connection with which are developed a large number of activities and feelings.

The great variety of block plays shows this same interest in construction. Some years ago I wanted to arrange some plays for my children which should make use of the desire to construct, but should not primarily involve finger movements and minute co-ordinations. I had blocks made large enough so that their use would involve arm movements. After some experiment I found that blocks about the size of bricks, twice as wide as they are thick and twice as long as they are wide, are more useful than any other shape. A thickness of one and a half inches allows a baby's hand to take a firm grasp. I had some three hundred wooden blocks made, all of this size, and gave them to the children.

For about six consecutive years those blocks were the chief interest of one or more of the children. An observation of the various structures made and the kind of buildings built showed that all the children went through the same general stages in block plays. The first step consisted in simply piling up the blocks and knocking them down. My boy did that more than any of the girls. Sometimes the children liked to lay the blocks in rows. But it was not until some time after they had begun playing with the blocks that they cared to have the corners fit and the angles placed accurately.

The interest in playing with the blocks was intense, but intermittent. The children never played with them for many weeks at a time. But as they grew older the period of their play impulse grew longer. A baby might play with the blocks every day for a little while; but a boy or girl of seven or eight played all day long for a number of days or a week, until that pulse of interest was exhausted. These bursts of interest were generally related to the discovery of

TOYS 71

some fresh form of construction. For instance, when the child first discovered the principle of balance which underlies bridge building, there was a very long pulse of interest. The children tried many kinds of bridges, until they had exhausted the form. When they received the notion of building houses, there was another period of interest, until they could discover no fresh varieties of house. They built as many kinds of houses as they could invent and then stopped. But they never completed a logical development of all the simple forms of block arrangement. They never, for instance, worked out all the possible relations of two blocks to each other. Their interests were grouped, not logically, but practically. The development of the consecutive forms of building, which has been similar with all the children, has not been logical. The particular form that the child happened to hit upon was executed in as many ways as he could think of.

The rôle of the teacher appears to come in when the child has exhausted his own ability to invent. As soon as he begins to do the same things over and over again, a teacher may suggest a new form. But the teacher who attempts to show all the forms to the child at once destroys the child's interest and renders him blasé.

To one of my children I showed in rapid succession all the generic forms of block arrangement—houses, bridges, mechanical forms. The child was too young to appreciate them, or to have any self-activity following the discovery. From that child I took away all the pleasure of block plays. I prevented him from developing his own instinct feelings in connection with his play. Nothing can so sap the interest and destroy the educative value of play so quickly as to discover everything for the child. This is the fault of the too complex toy. The chief value of any toy is that the boy can use it to do something with.

Self-development through playing is also brought about through the very limitations of material in these block plays. They were wooden blocks, all shaped alike. I might have given the children colored blocks of many shapes, German stone blocks with lintels, doorways and cupolas, so that building would have been easy and varied. But with the one shape of block the difference in construction lay in the imagination of the children rather than in the thing used. They developed a power of doing new things with old material, as they could never have done had they always had new material from the start. To a large extent independence, power, mastery over the material world, comes from using old things in new ways rather than from having the tool or the implement that is perfectly adapted to the present condition. In connection with these blocks, all the development seemed to lie in the imagination rather than in any new muscular co-ordinations. No special order of neuro-muscular development was noticeable in connection with the plays. But the blocks were used with increasing complexity, as imaginative material to represent trains or houses. Frequently a social play would be carried through with the use of the blocks as symbols, dividing one home from another.

The building of houses went through a definite evolution. At first the children were satisfied to make a pile of blocks and knock it down. Presently they began to prefer to make the pile straight and regular. They wanted the edges of the blocks to fit. Later they came to the idea of symmetry. They built their houses with a door on one side and a door on the other side, a window at this end and a window at that end. This second stage of æsthetic development is the stage in which many of us still find ourselves. We furnish our houses in this way, a rug here and a rug opposite; if there is a plate on the dining-room table on one side there must be a corresponding plate on the other side. But the children came in their block plays to the ideal of balance, which is a more profound æsthetic principle than that of symmetry. There was an endeavor to have balanced structures, not symmetrical, but proportioned. There were forts with their defenders; one or two houses for officers, a large three-story house. In all these ways the children went through a definite mental development, accomplished with the aid of blocks. Other toys may accomplish similar results if they give the child an opportunity to express his own activities. His personality must be allowed to develop through doing. This is not merely desirable for the child's education; it is necessary for his enjoyment of the play itself.

Doll play is a form of toy play in connection with which very complex mental and social developments take place. Dolls, like other toys, have their chief interest in the fact that they serve as instruments about which to cluster instinct feelings that need expression and development. In this case it is the domestic instincts that are ripening. Love grows not with the beauty and completeness of the doll, but with the amount of time and attention given to it by the girl. Hence arises the great affection which girls have for rag dolls. The rag doll gives more opportunity for work, and, therefore, more opportunity for the expression of affection. Many girls are exceedingly lonely without their dolls, but find a sufficient sense of companionship as soon as they have them, even if there are no human beings near. Girls talk to dolls extensively and tell them their troubles.

There are many kinds of dolls. Miss Maud Shipe tells of "flower dolls" with which she used to play. In a corner of the garden grew a number of old-fashioned flowers, petunias, zinnias, four-o'clocks, and phlox. The dolls were usually made with the half-opened bud of a zinnia for body. They were dressed in skirts made of petunias or four-o'clocks turned to show their brightest colors. Caps of salvia or verbena buds were worn. Men dolls were made of pinched-off stems of petunias, two serving for legs and a thicker one for the body. Sunflowers were dug out to form doll houses. For several years the children played dolls with these flowers, from early spring till late in the fall.

Another form of doll play was carried on in the orchard. Wild grass grew there, which branched out into thick tufts at the top. These tufts of grass were called the heads of children, and were braided into long plaits of "hair." This play was often very intricate, leading into many styles of hair-dressing. Sometimes the children were considered members of an orphan asylum, because there were so many of them.

Miss Shipe also developed at about the age of thirteen a complicated series of plays with paper dolls. The dolls themselves were very crude, cut out from folded paper, so that both sides were alike. They served merely as symbols around which to gather the complex series of relationships which the girls invented. There were large family organizations, with names and histories for each individual. There were houses, represented by strips of paper marking the walls, and furniture, consisting of labelled bits of paper. As the children played they kept up a kind of continued story, adding to it daily. They had weddings and funerals, visits, parties, Christmas dinners; and any event which once occurred was remembered and alluded to as part of the family history. The grown-up sons and daughters married and had children of their own so that at last there were two or three houses. Finally a church, a store, and a school were added to the now full-grown community.

The following year the dolls ceased to be used even as convenient symbols, but the continued story was kept up. This seems to show a regular progression from the simpler doll plays in which the actual doll was prominent, to the later plays, based on social relationships and domestic events, but no longer dependent even on the symbolic doll. In fact, Miss Shipe herself mentions such a progression, extending from a time preceding her play with paper dolls. She first played with regular dolls, gradually coming to prefer the smaller dolls because she "could do more things with them"; then her interest went to paper dolls cut from magazines and bearing an actual resemblance to people, and finally to the little paper dolls with round heads and bodies and long skirts, which served simply as symbols on which to hang a story. This is a natural progression, but it is by no means an inevitable one, as other girls tell of quite different experiences with dolls.

When one thinks of all the activities useful for later life that are first connected with dolls, the educational value of this form of play is not to be questioned. It takes in the whole problem of the making of clothing, the cutting, fitting, pattern-making, the ornamentation of dress, the use of color. So many persons learn these things later in life at very great expense, or to the humiliation of their parents, when they begin to dress themselves. My own girls acquired most of their knowledge of the relation of form to color, and styles of dress to the individual, through their play with dolls. I remember when the idea first came to the girls that there should be a connection between complexion and hats. Immediately they tried all shapes and sizes of hats to observe the effect. Those girls have an experience with reference to clothing which could have been secured in later life only with difficulty and expense.

The making of doll houses is also a play of educational value. One winter some of my children spent nearly three months making a doll's house with a complete set of doll furniture, sawed from designs. The wall-paper in the bedroom was ornamented with a pattern of sailing ships. The stove was complete with all cooking utensils. There were chairs of all patterns, some of them copied from an old museum near by. The children thus secured an idea of applied art. They learned the use of a color scheme in the rooms of houses, the use of design in architecture and furnishings.

Doll parties are occasions for learning a large part of the requirements of social life. Family relations and social customs are developed with increasing complexity. The doll plays may branch out into other related plays at about the age of twelve or thirteen, as was shown in the case of Miss Shipe's paper dolls. The dressing and undressing of dolls and the actual care of them come largely before this age. At this time most girls cease their most active playing with dolls and are more interested in babies and romances. Every one of our five children has been "borrowed" as a baby, to be trundled around by girls of thirteen and fourteen, not because our babies were particularly beautiful, but because the girls felt the need of something to care for. The doll was no longer satisfactory; they wanted something more real.

Ownership

Closely connected with the child's personal and social development are plays concerned with ownership. Part of the joy in making toys lies in the fact that the boy now has something which belongs to him, because he has created it, something which he can take about with him and show to other boys. But whether or not the child displays his possessions, and whether or not those possessions are toys, there is a very distinct joy in the mere sense of ownership. The first thing that I have a definite remembrance of owning was a pair of copper-toed boots. It was in July and exceedingly hot, and the boots were heavy and high. The only way in which I could be comfortable in those boots was to sit with my feet on the window sill in a draft. Nevertheless, they were my boots and I found joy in having them on, in spite of discomfort.

When my small boy began to realize that certain things belonged to him, he was not happy unless he could take them with him everywhere. At night he wanted all his own belongings in bed with him. He had a rag doll and an engine, and one or two crusts of bread which he saved, to take to bed. For a long time one of my daughters had the habit of hiding food in various places throughout the house. Pieces of bread, parts of bananas, anything that could be carried away unobserved from the table, were hidden behind screens and curtains and promptly forgotten. She was obeying an unusually strong instinct for the hoarding of possessions. There was no possibility of future lack; but she had the feeling nevertheless.

A small orphan was adopted into a home, coming from an asylum in which there was no individual ownership of property. The children had been adequately clothed, their beds were neat, and they had plenty of food; but they did not own anything. The first night when this child was put to bed in her new home, her garments were laid on a chair and she was told: "Those are your clothes. They will be put here so that you will find them in the morning." She did not seem to understand, but asked: "Shall I have them to-morrow?" "Yes, those are all your clothes." "Can I put them on the next day, too?" she asked. "Yes," she was told. She repeated the same questions about her shoes. "Are these all mine?" she asked. And then, when she was ready for bed, she took all the clothes into her arms. They were the first things that child had ever owned in her life.

Ownership is closely related to development of personality. We shall never know how to treat possessions that we have in common until we have a high sense of personal ownership. The person who owns nothing is irresponsible. We are, indeed, training children to live in a social world. The sky and the trees are general property. We are increasingly owning many things through community partnership—schools, parks, playgrounds. But the relation of the child to school property, school text-books, school furniture, shows how slowly the sense of personal responsibility attaches itself to objects owned in common. The feeling may be developed and should be. But it will be developed more easily by recognizing the sense of individual proprietorship than by violating this feeling. The sense of ownership is very strong and fundamental. The boy who owns a stamp-album and loses it through the thieving instincts of another boy feels that his personality has been outraged. His feeling is quite different from that which he instinctively has when school property is disturbed; though, later in life, with the dawn of class and school loyalty, the feeling for the banners, trophies, and other possessions of his class may come to be even stronger than was the earlier individual feeling. But the later sense of common ownership is developed through the sense of individual ownership. . Personal responsibility is not adequately developed unless the child has the opportunity to own things, to trade with them, to have and exercise the sense of possession.

CHAPTER VII

MASCULINE AND FEMININE DIFFERENCES

IN the discussion of plays, recollections come to each of us which depend largely on whether we are men or women. My first vivid memory of my relation to a doll centred about the time when my sister had a party and asked me to go up-stairs to bring down her doll. It was a large doll, and, with a small boy's ingenuity, I tied a string around its neck and attached the other end to a broomstick, and so came into the room dragging the doll. My sister's actions at the sight showed that her feelings toward that doll were very different from mine.

There are, on the other hand, many plays which are pre-eminently boys' plays and possess relatively small interest for girls. The hunting and fighting plays come under this head. Boys compete more than girls. Competition is an ever-present element in their lives. For this reason they are accustomed to take defeat better than girls. When twenty boys run in a race, only one can win. It is a rare boy who is ahead of his fellows most of the time. Boys learn to accept these facts. On the other hand, I have seen the most cultivated and mature young women lose complete control of themselves and their tempers over a decision in a game of basket-ball. Women do not enjoy competition in the same way as men do. Even in adults the possession of the fighting instinct is one of the differentiations between men and women. There are two sparrows fighting; men like it, women do not. There is a spontaneous dog fight. Men gather around it; no women will be found there. Men may stop the fight, but while it lasts it holds their interest.

The desire to throw straight and hard seems to be an instinctively masculine desire. It is not because of man's special adaptability that he is able to throw better than a woman. A man's shoulder-joint is not very different from a woman's. In fact, what differences there are in the joint itself seem to be in favor of the woman. But the man has a better neural coordination, a different instinct feeling about throwing. Because girls do not have this ideal about throwing hard and straight they do not play the competitive games of boys which require this special ability.

SEX DIFFERENCES

Girls have, however, plays which are peculiarly their own. Many years ago, when my first daughter was born, my wife and I planned for her a childhood which should omit dolls. Most of the disorders in my family had been of a nervous type—headaches, earaches, backaches, rather than any organic troubles—and we wished our children to be out of doors a great deal in order to counteract this tendency. So we encouraged our daughter in all forms of boys' plays, and gave her much opportunity for playing outdoor games. We gave her no dolls, because dolls lead to sedentary occupation. We decided that she should not play indoors with other girls, for we feared that through such association the habit of doll play would be acquired. She was not taken down-town to the shops where dolls are prominently displayed lest she should be attracted by them. The plan seemed to work very well for a few years. But one Christmas she was asked what gift she wanted more than anything else. To the astonishment and confusion of her parents she answered: "Oh, if I could only have a doll." She received that doll and so did the three sisters who came after her.

Some years afterward I took a doll census and discovered that there were in the house thirty-seven members of the doll family, each with its own name and relationships. That number did not include the clothes-pin dolls, spool dolls, paper dolls, dolls made from acorns, or any other of the great community of ephemeral dolls that come and go. It included only the regularly established members of the household. These girls had no more intense relations to dolls than most girls have. A remarkable development of domestic feeling was brought about in connection with this doll family. Doll play is essentially girl play. Much of the rich, social life of women and the ready use of the hands come through playing with dolls. The manual skill that boys acquire is different in kind.

Some boys play with dolls in much the same way as girls do. But usually when boys play with dolls, the military or pedagogical side is emphasized. Many boys have armies and a great many play school with dolls. Every toy store has different forms of boys' dolls, tin-soldiers, lead-soldiers, with guns for shooting them. Boys have been known to make soldiers out of screws and spools and pieces of elastic. The boy's toys are usually just as definitely related to man's activities as the domestic doll play is to woman's activity.

The difference is, of course, one of emphasis

only. During those years in which dolls were of predominant interest, my girls also played hide-and-seek and various outdoor games. They played these games well, but did not find them ultimately satisfying. During those same years of childhood many boys play with dolls. But the games which predominate among boys are not built upon the domestic instinct; they are built rather upon the fighting and hunting instincts.

The same difference in instincts is evident in adult life. The father's feeling toward his children is quite different from the mother's. I remember watching my wife rocking an infant daughter. She was singing to the child with such manifest delight, such deep-seated satisfaction in the outgoing of affection, that I wished to experience the same enjoyment. I learned the same song and held the baby in the same way, but I did not have the same feeling. My whole attitude was different. The fundamental mistake lay in trying to duplicate the woman's relations to the baby. The paternal instinct may be as strong as the maternal, but it is different.

Several statements received from teachers with regard to the kinds of play observed by them among girls and boys show a striking one-

88 A PHILOSOPHY OF PLAY

ness in their conclusions. The details of their statements may not be universally applicable, but will serve to show the general distinctions in play. Miss Helen Frances Doherty, for instance, noted the following differences between boys and girls. Boys have many muscular plays, wrestling and fighting; girls have social plays, calling and visiting. Boys have the constructive impulse toward large things, such as hut-building; girls like to construct minute things, such as patterns. Boys are more anxious than girls to try new things; they show a love of the grotesque as opposed to the love of the conventional shown by girls. Boys endure dress for utilitarian reasons only; girls love dress for æsthetic reasons. Boys play more often in gangs, girls in pairs. Among boys a quarrel leads to a fight, among girls to pouting and mean remarks. Boys like to shock, or expressing the same instinct in another way, to excite admiration for feats they perform. Girls like to act shocked and to admire.

These same differences appear in other relations besides those of play. In school life boys seem to be more loyal to one another than girls are. Boys who get into a scrape, and even other boys who merely know about the scrape, will stand punishment and expulsion from school for not telling. Sometimes such cases occur among girls, but it is the general testimony of the teachers with whom I have talked that boys are far more loyal to one another than girls are.

These masculine and feminine differences may no doubt be based to a certain extent on social tradition. Girls can learn to play basket-ball, though it is the almost universal opinion of those who have coached girls that they acquire the habits of team-play less readily than do boys. Certain changes can no doubt be made in the accepted traditions of girls' and boys' play. But upon the whole, these differences are so fundamental and show themselves so spontaneously, that we seem driven to the conclusion that they are based upon different instinct feelings.

Certain great ideals have always had a place in the human mind. Long before the dawn of history they were bound up in the texture of our nature; they became ingrained facts. In women, one of these ideals is loyalty to the home; in men, loyalty to the tribe. Necessity produced these ideals. They have a survival value. The very existence of the race required this double set of loyalty impulses. To a certain extent they have been safeguarded by instinct; to an even greater extent social tradition has become sponsor for them. The deepest disgrace to a woman has always been disloyalty to the home; the deepest disgrace to a man has been disloyalty to his tribe, or his country.

We have already noticed the fact that the men who were the best runners, fighters, and hunters, were best equipped to survive in the struggle for existence. For this reason the boys who loved to fight, hunt, and run, and therefore played at all these activities, grew into the men who survived. This is true also of the higher development of the fighting feeling into the spirit of loyalty for a group. With a man his tribe counted first. His home life was a matter of comparatively little moment; his wife was his property, to do with as he chose. In tribal affairs the principle of every man for himself meant disaster. A man standing alone was an easy mark for enemies—human beings, or wild beasts, or unharnessed forces of nature. Fighting, hunting, and working in gangs was the only feasible schedule for such unprotected creatures. Men had to stand together.

This is the basis of the gang instinct which becomes so prominent among boys in their teens. It is also the basis for the intense interest taken in team games and interschool athletics. These athletic competitions cannot be defended on the ground of physical training, for they train only a small proportion of the boys, and particularly those individuals who are least in need of training. Their real justification is in the spirit of athletics, the loyalty to school, the social consciousness which includes in its grasp all the students, not merely those who actually compete. The effect of school athletics on school spirit and on the boy's recognition of his share in a larger whole was illustrated by the statement of a boy on the East Side of New York. "Our school wasn't nothin' at all till we got a gym," he said. "Now we're the champions." It was well for that boy to realize his partnership in a group; it was the beginning of training in wider loyalty.

It is not sufficient in the cultivation of any virtue to give maxims or formal instruction. In looking for the beginnings of social morality, we must discover the elements in boy character. The strongest instinct which may be utilized for this purpose is the gang instinct, and one of the most wholesome forms of gang activity is in athletic team sports. The gang is a manifestation of group loyalty. It is true that in most of our large cities the tendency of the gang is evil, because the major part of its activities is, and almost must be, against the social order. It is the function of school athletics, when rightly conducted, to convert this gang instinct from evil into righteousness. Social education is going on with all boys; we must see to it that the education is good. The gang is the modern representative of the tribe, the germ out of which the club and society develop. By being loyal to the gang, and having the gang clean and moral, by being loyal to the class and school, the qualities of social morality and social conscience are being developed. This is essentially the root of masculine altruism.

The development of women has been different. They were not predominantly hunters or fighters, but cared for the home and carried on the industries. They wove the cloth, made the baskets, tilled the soil, cared for the domestic animals, reared the children, made the clothing, and performed the numerous other duties that centred around the home. Running, throwing, and striking were not the chief measures of their usefulness. The women who were the best mothers, who were the most true to their homes, were the women whose children survived. So it is clear that athletics have never been either a test or a large factor in the survival of women; athletics do not test womanliness as they test manliness.

SEX DIFFERENCES

An illustration of this fact came to my attention on the occasion of a field-day meet for its girls held by one of our New York City high schools. There were seven events, held under conditions which were practically the same as the conditions for events that are annually held at Vassar College. The high school girls on their first field-day made better records in four events than had ever been made by the students of Vassar College. That is, progress toward womanhood had not meant progress toward increased efficiency in athletic sports. In basketball it is not at all uncommon for a team of girls of about twelve years to defeat a team of young women of college age. The little girls are more athletic. Their bodies have not yet differentiated into the form of the adult woman.

The women of the world have never played team-games. They are beginning to play them now. But hitherto their road to altruism and the larger devotion to the whole has been the road of the home. The history of the development of the family and of the instinct feelings that lead to domestic life shows that out of the love and self-sacrifice of mothers for their children has grown a large part of the spirit of service which is coming to be more and more characteristic of the best of mankind. Studies in the development of the higher moral ideals of men, made by Geddes, Sutherland, Drummond, and Fiske, have endeavored even to show that all of altruism has grown out of the love of mothers for their children.

The domestic instincts of women are closely connected with the girl's manner of play. A study was made in a mothers' club in regard to the doll plays of its members during their childhood. Each member wrote down, as completely as her memory allowed, a history of her play with dolls. She recorded not merely the material facts about the dolls, but the various ways in which she had played with them, their domestic relations, sicknesses, mental and moral characteristics. She recorded also her own feelings about the dolls, how they arose, how long they lasted, how strong they were. These women also wrote out, as honestly as they could, something about the facility with which they had come into the new relations of motherhood and the tasks of the home, their feelings regarding housework, its daily drudgery, and the care of children. It was the unanimous agreement of this group of mothers that, on the whole, those women who during childhood had played most fully with their dolls, came into the relations of domestic life with a feeling of greater ease and enjoyment than did those to whom doll play had been less important.

This does not, of course, mean that doll play produces domestic feelings, but it does seem to indicate that doll play and domestic feelings are related. It seems to show that doll play is the budding forth of those same instincts which show themselves later in the domestic relations of life. Moreover, the doll play has an effect in establishing the domestic instincts by giving them opportunity for normal development when they first appear. The tender care of the sick doll, the making of clothes for the doll, the study of color schemes, the sense of the significance of social customs gained at dolls' parties—in these and a hundred other ways the child acquires by simple and wholesome development a knowledge of the things which are essential in life. It does not seem that this knowledge can be gained so readily where that preliminary education which comes through doll play is lacking.

Nor is it merely, or chiefly, a question of intellectual knowledge. It must not be inferred from anything that has been said that a woman who has never played with dolls cannot, by taking courses in domestic art and domestic science, and by faithful attendance on lectures, learn to do all that a woman in domestic life should do. But our adaptability to the kind of work that we have to do is not chiefly a question of intellectual adaptability. It is mainly an adjustment of our liking and disliking, and turns upon the question of whether or not we enjoy doing that thing. Do we enter upon it with ease and freedom? Does it appeal to us as lovable in itself? To establish the instinctive love of home and children so deeply that the feeling will last through the drudgery of the work involved, this is part of the function of doll play.

So the love of dolls, with all of its wonderfully complex development, is not merely a pastime. It is one of the main agencies for developing the higher instinct feelings of girls. In the kindergarten and the lower grades of the elementary school there should be doll plays, with dolls belonging to individual girls—thus giving them the opportunity of developing the feelings toward home, shelter, and children. These feelings are just now in peculiar danger of perversion or lack of development, owing to the change in the family home under modern city conditions. Girls in tenements and apartments have far less opportunity for the growth of domestic feelings than is afforded to girls in homes. Whether the life of the adult is to be peculiarly domestic in nature or not, these domestic feelings need development, since they are one of the great roots of altruism. We cannot produce these feelings, but we can give them an opportunity to grow.

SEX DIFFERENCES

The important question is raised whether it may not be true that, in view of the wide competition into which women are coming in the modern world, it would be wise for them to have the discipline afforded by athletic sports. This may be true to a certain extent. The question whether young women shall play competitive games hinges on the question of what woman is going to be. If the states of mind involved in basket-ball are related to the states of mind desirable for women, then basket-ball is good. Indiscriminate basket-ball is certainly bad. Home basket-ball is good. The ground between the two is debatable. If we want women who can co-operate, who can compete, we shall not find these qualities in the scholastic activities. Basket-ball may be a special element in the education of the new woman.

During the modern age men are acquiring the virtues which have always been predominantly feminine—chastity, love of children, patience, loyalty to home. Women, on the other hand, are beginning to be loyal to one another in a new way. Women's clubs all over the civilized world show that it is possible for women to work successfully together. Women are beginning to show a profound interest in the community and the state. The virtues demanded of both men and women are getting to be more nearly identical than they have been in the past. But it does not seem likely that the paths by which men and women reach the final goal of devotion to the common good will ever be the same paths. The fundamental qualities to be cultivated in the boy are those of muscular strength, the despising of pain, driving straight to the mark, and the smashing down of obstacles. The world needs power and the barbaric virtues of manhood, together with the type of group loyalty which is based upon these savage virtues. It needs also the gentler virtues of the love of home, kindness, sympathy, and forbearance. Both men and women need a share in all these virtues, but the order in which they acquire them, and the roads by which they attain the desired ends are diverse. What these roads are is best seen in a study of the spontaneous plays of boys and girls.

CHAPTER VIII
THE PLAY OF ANIMALS

I WENT repeatedly to Prospect Park to study the crowd that was watching three young bears at play. It was a crowd full of keen interest to see what the little bears would do, as they rolled over one another, played informal tag, or climbed the miniature trees placed in their den. There is no cage in the zoological garden more constantly watched than the cage which contains a large group of young foxes, bears, or members of the cat tribe. A litter of puppies that have become active is exceedingly interesting. A family of young cats affords entertainment to all who come.

The play life of young animals begins very early. If by play we mean those actions that are done instinctively with no immediate purpose we must include some strange things. Lloyd Morgan tells of the chirping of chicks within the shell, before hatching. He says:[1] "Young moor-hens chirp in some cases for more than forty-eight hours, and ducklings as

[1] C. Lloyd Morgan, *Habit and Instinct*, Edward Arnold, London and New York, 1896, page 31.

many as twenty-four hours, before they emerge." This is a common phenomenon and one which I have myself observed with a brood of chicks. Moreover, the fear caused by the parent bird's warning begins to manifest itself even before the young are hatched. This prenatal "peeping" stops at once if the mother utters the warning note even at a considerable distance.

Can instances of this kind be rightly included in the category of play? Do they have the same relation to adult life that other recognized forms of play have? A consideration of some less questioned forms of animal play is the only answer to this question. The playing of kittens with balls dragged in front of them, and the playing of dogs with bones, are instances of the often-noticed sportive activities of domestic animals.

A friend who had a large family of cats has described some of their plays in detail. She declares that they vary individually in their play, just as they vary in other habits. But their plays all bear some relation to the activities by which they gain their livelihood as adults. "The mother and grandmother of them all and her brother Peter were the most playful kittens I have ever seen," she says. "They used to begin at daylight, and they had to be shut up in the evening while the chickens went to roost, because they would chase them so that they could not get settled. Even now the old mother plays sometimes with a string or stick, although she tires more quickly. She is the best mouser we have ever had." The connection here between the early play and the later ability to catch mice is worth noting.

Kilter was from a family of mousers. He had several original ways of playing. He would take a piece of meat and worry it as if it were a mouse, while Xantippe, a kitten from another family in the house, could never be taught to play in that fashion. Kilter used to take a small object in his mouth, stand up on a chair or couch, let the plaything roll over the edge, and then go for it. He would play that way for half an hour or more at a time. Other cats seemed less definite in their play, and used most of their energy in chasing one another, running about very rapidly, and climbing trees. They would often lie down in a path and roll over and over.

W. H. Hudson has described the play of the puma, which he characterizes as the "most playful animal in existence." He says: "It is at heart always a kitten, taking unmeasured delight in its frolics; and when, as often happens, one lives alone in the desert, it will amuse it-

102   A PHILOSOPHY OF PLAY

self by the hour fighting mock battles or playing at hide-and-seek with imaginary companions. I was told by one person who had spent most of his life on the pampas that on one occasion he had seen four pumas playing. It was at nine o'clock in the evening and a bright moon was shining. He was lying quietly in the shelter of a rock. After a while they began to gambol together close to him, concealing themselves from one another among the rocks, just as kittens do, and then pursuing one another."[1]

A consecutive record of the development of the play life of several individual animals has been made by Wesley Mills. He has recorded the day-by-day growth of puppies and kittens. In one litter of puppies, he observed the play between two puppies on the fifteenth day, and found that paws and jaws both were being used. Two days later playing was more common. He adds: "Slight movements of the tail are noticed during play, and there is an obvious increase in walking power; muscular co-ordinations of all kinds are better made." On the thirty-third day, when put on the floor of the kennel, they do not manifest uneasiness, but run about and play. "One is seen to run at a slow rate, with his tail

[1] W. H. Hudson, *The Naturalist in La Plata*, Chapman & Hall, Ltd., London, 1892, page 40.

THE PLAY OF ANIMALS

up, and several make quick starts backward and forward."

Mr. Mills goes on to say:

"Much of the play of dogs is mimic fighting, even from the first, and I have noted on the twenty-seventh day, during a play, a very brief but decided exhibition of anger, such as may occasionally be seen among mature dogs, or among boys of eight or nine years during rough play. The length of time which this anger lasts depends greatly on the breed of the dog. With terriers very early play becomes serious at times, and later there may be so much fighting that these dogs cannot with safety be left together. In few respects do the different breeds show their characteristics at so early an age as in this. . . .

"Suggestive action, especially in connection with play, has a very important share in determining the direction of development, and the manner of individual the dog becomes. It is very common from the fortieth day onward, and greatly increases the activity and hastens the progress of the members of a litter, as compared with a single young dog kept apart. It often, I have noticed, advances a puppy of a few months to a place with older dogs; and this is sometimes followed by the best physical, as well as psychic results, especially if the young dog be allowed to go out to exercise with the older ones. Suggestive action may also have an evil effect on young dogs. Much of the sheep-worrying results from it. . . ."[1]

[1] Wesley Mills, *The Nature and Development of Animal Intelligence*, The Macmillan Co., New York, 1908, pages 122, 123, 133, 159, 163, 216.

"A certain mongrel brought up alone seemed to be very slow in developing the play instinct, which I attribute largely to his being the sole puppy from an early period, and therefore seeing no other dog but his dam."[1]

There is a great difference in the various instincts with reference to their development through play. Flying, for instance, seems to be acquired by birds without teaching, simply through the ripening of instincts. William James has made a very interesting experiment in this direction. Strings were tied around the wings of some members of a nestful of birds and they were replaced in the nest. The other birds were left free. In the course of time the free birds learned to fly. Then the strings were removed from the tied birds and it was discovered that they could fly equally well. Whether the ripening of instincts was in itself sufficient, or whether the presence of an example was necessary, was of course not decided by this experiment, but it proved at least that little definite practice was essential.

In order to become personally acquainted with the consecutive history of the play life of certain animals I kept guinea-pigs, ferrets, cats,

[1] Wesley Mills, *The Nature and Development of Animal Intelligence*, The Macmillan Co., New York, 1908, pages 216, 226, 231.

THE PLAY OF ANIMALS 105

dogs, birds, chickens, and other animals, and made notes of their daily activities. I endeavored to watch the development of play in the individual animal, to note differences between individuals in the same family, and between different types of animals. Inasmuch as this volume is a study of human play, it does not seem worth while to do more than give certain general conclusions with reference to these observations.

An illuminating contrast appears in comparing the play activities of two such animals as the guinea-pig and the dog. I watched a young guinea-pig from the moment of birth to adult life and found no activities that could be surely described as play. The young guinea-pig appeared to be able to care for itself immediately after birth. Its reactions were relatively complete from the start. With the dog it is quite different. A new-born puppy, while not as helpless as the human baby, is quite dependent upon the parent. It is unable to walk or to care for itself in any way. The consecutive activities of the puppy appeared in rather regular order, the impulse of play being intense though periodic. The general conclusion seems to be that the complexity of the play life of all the animals I observed was a direct measure of the intelligence of the species as a whole and the individual in particular.

Different individuals show great contrasts in their play life. This relates to the vigor with which they play, the amount of time they spend in play, the quickness with which they imitate the mother and develop initiative. There is also a difference in species. The play life of the cat has certain marked resemblances to and certain marked differences from the play life of the dog. The dog is more imitative; the behavior of one kitten has little influence on the behavior of another. This is closely related to the fact that dogs, when grown, hunt in packs and associate much more readily than do cats. The type of hunting shown by the cat in play, the lying-in-wait, the crouching, is very imperfectly developed in the dog. It never becomes his peculiar manner of hunting. The dog is a social animal, while the cat is unsocial or even anti-social. All these qualities appear in their play life.

Ernest Thompson Seton has given several accounts of the play of wild foxes. The following is one of these tales, showing the way in which the young learn through play the activities which will be of use later.

"They played about, basking in the sun, or wrestling with each other, till a slight sound made them scurry underground. Their alarm was needless, for the cause of it was their mother. She stepped from the bushes, bringing them another hen—number seventeen, as I remember. A low call from her, and the little fellows came tumbling out. They rushed on the hen, and tussled and fought with it and each other, while their mother, keeping a sharp eye out for enemies, looked on with fond delight. . . . The base of my tree was hidden in bushes and much lower than the knoll where the fox was. So I could come and go at will without scaring them. For many days I saw much of the training of the young ones. They early learned to turn to statuettes at any strange sound, and then on hearing it again or finding other cause for fear, to run for shelter." [1]

Still another account of young foxes describes the way in which they learned to seize and devour woodchucks in which life was not yet entirely extinct. They growled and fought with all the strength of their baby jaws, until the woodchuck got away. Then it was promptly brought back by the mother, who carefully refrained from killing it herself. "Again and again this rough sport went on till one of the little ones was badly bitten, and his squeal of pain roused the mother to end the woodchuck's misery and serve him up at once." Later the mother took the four foxes out to hunt fieldmice. They used the tactics they had already

[1] Ernest Thompson Seton, *Wild Animals I Have Known*, Charles Scribner's Sons, New York, 1900, page 197.

108 A PHILOSOPHY OF PLAY

acquired in play. Mr. Seton adds: "When at length the eldest for the first time in his life caught game, he quivered with excitement and ground his pearly, milk-white teeth into the mouse with a rush of inborn savageness." [1]

Much additional knowledge is needed before our grasp of the subject of animal play is even partially satisfactory. We need more records of the play life of single animals that shall show the amount and character of their play. It is not sufficient for us to know that these animals occasionally perform certain actions. We must know to what extent the actions are common; how much time is spent on them. We need careful observations of the character of this play, and its relation to the adult activities of the same species. Does the play life of the young foreshadow the life of the adult animal? We can trace some connection between the two, but for accurate and detailed conclusions we need far more extended observations than we have now.

We need observations of animals kept apart from other animals of the same kind, to see how much of their play life is purely instinctive and how much is derived from others—parents or comrades. We need to compare the develop-

[1] *Ibid.*, page 204.

THE PLAY OF ANIMALS 109

ment of those kept by themselves and those brought up by their parents. We need to observe carefully in such animals as the cat and the dog, where it is most easy, the part taken by the parents in teaching the young to play, and the apparent psychic state of the parent while the young are playing. Other problems may also be solved by careful observation. How much exercise does a puppy get in an hour of play? What kind of exercise? What parts of his body are brought into activity? Are his senses involved much? What is the nature of the motor training in his play? How long will he play? Does this vary at different ages? The kind of observation one gives to animals ordinarily is very different from the kind given when endeavoring to answer specific questions such as these. We need more data from patient, unprejudiced observation.

The observations already recorded serve to show the wide extent of the play life among living beings. It extends from creatures of very low intelligence to man, from infancy to old age. Several other conclusions may also be reached with more or less definiteness.

In so far as the young of animals have any physical training at all, or any of the exercise necessary to growth, it is secured through play.

They have no serious exercises, undertaken for the sake of muscular development. They go out to play because they like it. By this means they obtain all the motor and muscular training they receive.

The plays of animals are related to their race habits. The instincts needed in later life seem to be expressed and developed in play. In the case of domesticated animals, the play life seems to express the instincts needed by the animal in a wild state. The complexity of the play life of any group of young animals seems to be a measure of their capacity for intelligence. The play of a dog, for instance, is infinitely more complicated than that of a fish. The plays of dogs are more social than those of cats, for the dog belongs to the pack family. His chief attachment is to his kind. Thus, in many ways, the plays of the young animals relate themselves to the adult life of their kind.

In a given species the various plays seem to present a definitely co-ordinated series of activities, each one built upon the preceding one, as definitely as long division is built upon addition, subtraction, and multiplication. The order of development is from the simple to the complex, from the racially elementary to that which is recent; from the muscularly and neurally funda-

THE PLAY OF ANIMALS 111

mental to that which is accessory. Among animals which play social plays, these come later in time than the individual plays. A dog learns to manage himself before he plays games of a social character. Mastery of self must, in the nature of the case, precede co-operation.

It is also evident that tradition and example are necessary parts of animal play, especially among the more intelligent animals. Both dogs and cats want to hunt, but they learn to hunt in the precise way in which the instinct is shaped by the parents. Small terriers brought up by a cat and taught in the cat manner of hunting have been known to lie down in front of a mouse hole and remain perfectly motionless, waiting for a mouse. This is an example of the way in which instinct is shaped by tradition. The dog would not have hunted at all if he had not possessed the instinct, but precept gave him the method of hunting. Birds do not learn to sing without suggestion. They do not make the characteristic nests of their species without seeing the nests made. The larger part of the traditions necessary to adult activity are practised in play when the animal is young.

When one watches an animal at play now and then, its play seems random, just as the play of boys and girls appears to one who sees it now and then. But when one observes more carefully and sees the tremendous story of the great sequences of physical, social, and mental development suggested by the sequences of play, then one becomes fascinated by its complexity. The whole adult life, not only of the individual, but also of the species, is closely akin to the life of play.

CHAPTER IX
THE PLAY OF ADULTS

IF it were possible to make an instantaneous census at nine o'clock some Saturday evening, recording the age, sex, and occupation of every person in a given district, it would be of the utmost value for a study of many problems of modern life. I select Saturday evening because it is the time most devoted to purposes of recreation and play. A census of this kind would show how many people are at that time on the streets, how many are in saloons, how many are in billiard halls, how many in bowling-alleys, how many in gymnasiums, in dance-halls, in theatres, at lectures. We should know thus what use is being made of leisure time throughout a given district, could estimate what proportion of people is being strengthened and rested by it, and what proportion is degrading body and soul through amusement.

We have a fairly accurate knowledge of the working life of a modern city, and in fact of the entire country. We know how many people are engaged in the iron trade, how many are miners, or engineers, and how many are employed on farms. We know something concerning the food and shelter obtained by various classes of people. But we have no knowledge of how many people dance, or how many are interested in art or philosophy. We have very little idea of what people do when they are pleasing themselves and following their own ideas of a "good time." Such a census would tell us more concerning the mental and moral conditions of the district investigated than almost any other records could give.

I tried at one time to get an estimate of the amount of money spent in America on recreation. I secured a few items like the following. In 1904 we spent nearly $3,000,000 on our great baseball leagues. This does not include the money spent on smaller leagues and on balls and bats for children's games. In another year over $10,000,000 were spent by our men in hunting. The amount spent incidentally is not included.

Yachting is only one of the sports of our country. Counting only the large boats, there were 2,959 vessels of all sizes and descriptions. Of these 516 were steamers, 367 gas-engine or electric-motor boats, 205 schooners, 136 catboats. The total value of these pleasure boats

THE PLAY OF ADULTS 115

amounted to more than $40,000,000. This includes only the large, registered ships. The tens of thousands of small boats which the rest of us had were not counted, and it is probable that they also represented over $40,000,000. Play is not an incidental activity of adult life. It is to be reckoned as one of the great expenses of a nation.

There were in 1906 in New York City, 450 moving-picture shows with an average daily attendance at each of 1,000 persons. That made 450,000 persons per day taking part in this one form of public amusement. On Sunday these shows had an average attendance of 540,000. These plays are usually less objectionable from a moral standpoint than many people suppose; but the exhibitions have no value as exercise, and the ventilation is so inadequate that an hour spent in one of these halls, with the attendant risk of exposure to contagious disease, is a positive menace to health.

New York had in the same year about 200 dance-halls, nearly all of them connected with saloons. Dancing is in itself a thoroughly wholesome form of recreation and exercise; but the moral environment of those places of amusement was such that it is not pleasant to think that many of the future mothers of American children were resorting to them to satisfy the natural cravings for play and companionship. It is not necessary to mention the saloons and other resorts in our large cities which, under the guise of affording amusement, are inflicting evil upon our young people. Moreover, few of us realize to what an extent some of our national institutions, such as the Fourth of July, have become sources of bodily harm because of our inexcusable way of letting things take care of themselves. The intelligent direction which these celebrations require would not only rob them of their capacity to injure, but would vastly enhance their ability to do good.

Why do we play? That is a question which can be finally considered only from an ultimate philosophical standpoint. But there are several reasons which are readily apparent. In play we tend to balance the specialization of our work life. A man who works almost exclusively with his brain, will rarely have recreation of the same type; and he should not. He should play golf, row, swim, run, shoot, take care of horses. These plays tend to exercise otherwise unused parts of the body and of the mind as well; and to do this is the usual tendency of play. Yet this principle holds good only within limits. The men who work predominantly with the

THE PLAY OF ADULTS 117

muscular system make use of it also in their plays. The recreations of men who load steamers or of those who dig ditches are apt to be wrestling, dancing, and other forms of muscular activity. If play were merely the exercise of functions not used in work, we should have our manual workers studying philosophy during their hours of rest.

Play reproduces the earlier, simpler racial reactions. In golf we have the old feeling of hitting hard and straight; in hunting, the old outdoor relations. The taking care of a garden, in which so many people find real recreation, is a survival of the simpler, more primitive, agricultural activities.

Most modern city activities involve new adjustments of our neuro-muscular apparatus. They are much more specialized than the tasks to which our nervous systems have been accustomed in the past history of the race. A man cannot dictate letters for as many hours as he can hunt. In writing, he is making new demands on his nervous system, he is working with machinery not yet fully suited to its task. When he is fatigued by these recently acquired activities, he finds rest in reverting to older and more perfectly organized activities. A man fatigued by intellectual work may go to bed, but he will probably get more rest by walking a long distance, by playing golf, working with horses and dogs, by using reflexes that have been employed so long in the life of the race that they do not demand conscious attention. To go out and walk in the woods, to hear the birds, to listen to the babble of the water and the roar of the storm, to prepare food at a camp fire—by doing these old, old things we restore to ourselves the energy which we lose in the exercise of the recently acquired activities.

The will becomes easily fatigued under the strain of constant attention. When we let go of the will and act under the influence of caprice, we tend to revert to the older, more elementary activities. And when we have rested well in the summer, our wills are far more able to take hold of work in the fall than they were in the spring. For this reason also our tempers are probably better in the fall than in the spring. By reversion not merely to muscular activities of any kind, but to muscle relations and psychic activities that are old, by doing things that are done without consciously strained attention, we rest our wills.

The things we do when we are free to do what we please are vitally related to both health and morality. Those nations which devoted their

THE PLAY OF ADULTS 119

leisure to the recreating of health and the building up of beautiful bodies have tended to survive, while those which turned to dissipation in the marginal hours have written for us the history of national downfall. A daily life in which there is no opportunity for recreation may be fraught with as much evil as leisure time given over to a futile frittering away of energy. Time for rest and recreation is an absolute necessity for personal development; it is especially necessary under modern industrial conditions, where work of a peculiarly fatiguing nature is carried on. When a man works twelve hours in a steel mill, as we are told was the practice in Pittsburg, this condition is not merely significant from the standpoint of physical overwork; it is significant also from the standpoint of the family. A man so situated has neither strength nor time for recreation, nor for pursuing any of those ideals on which family life is built.

The importance of having some leisure time is no greater than that of the proper use of this time. An investigation in England showed that the effect of shortening the day of anthracite coal-miners from eight to six hours resulted in a lessened output per hour. During their leisure time the men dissipated so much that they were less competent in working hours. The important fact to be noticed is not mainly the lessened productive activity, but the reason for it, which led to the degeneration of the workers. It is a commonly observed fact that Monday is a bad day in many if not most industries, and it is bad because of the unwise use made of the leisure time on Sunday.

The recreation problem ranks in importance with the labor and education problems. Character is made predominantly during leisure hours. During work or school time our actions are guided by others. In recreation we do as we please. It is true that honesty in business and faithfulness in work are important elements in the making of character, but the great bulk of crime to-day, and the greatest part of the degeneration during all the eras of history, has resulted from wrong play and recreation, rather than through work.

The companions I choose during my leisure are more important with reference to the development of character than are my associates during business hours. With the latter I am forced to work; but if, after business is over, I choose men and women of fine personality, wholesome desires, and good tastes, my choice reflects my own self and tends to produce good character in me. If I deliberately associate

THE PLAY OF ADULTS 121

with men and women who disregard the higher sanctions of life, it indicates and tends to produce bad character. The choices we make with reference to our leisure are fundamental for morality. In the city, people have small opportunity to make this choice under wholesome conditions.

A young man of my acquaintance who came to the city went to one of the common dance-halls. I asked him why. He said: "I am alone. I wanted to see some girls. I have no opportunity to meet any. Why shouldn't I go?" The desire to see a young woman is a wholesome one, and it uplifts or degrades, according to the character of the girl; yet in New York City, by failing to make any provision for this instinct which is basic to community life, we have allowed it to be exploited commercially in saloon dance-halls, so that it acts almost wholly on the side of evil and immorality.

Restrictive measures are not adequate to the need. The attitude usually taken by the state with reference to public recreation is one of restriction only. We do little toward providing forms of play for social life; only when the saloon has grown to be sufficiently evil do we take steps to restrict it. When the theatre becomes sufficiently immoral, we make restrictions there also. When the moving-picture show becomes objectionable, we attempt to regulate it. When the dance-halls become too notoriously numerous as attachments to saloons and places of immorality, we pass restrictive measures. This is no doubt necessary, but it cannot solve the problem of adequate play for adults. It is not enough to tell the moving-picture managers that they must not do certain things. It would be well to tell them in positively constructive ways what they can do, for in itself the moving-picture show affords opportunity for wholesome recreation and education as well.

The same is true of the dance-hall. The dancing is in itself not only innocent, but good exercise. Its surroundings are often bad. Constructive measures are needed rather than purely restrictive ones. This applies to any form of recreation. It has even happened that certain playgrounds have become sources of evil, so that measures of doing away with them had to be enacted. What was needed was constructive work which would not only prevent those playgrounds from becoming headquarters of neighborhood toughs, but which would make them useful as the headquarters of the children's play.

Financial problems are not primary in these

THE PLAY OF ADULTS

considerations. The first need is that many people shall give thought to these matters. We have enormous resources belonging to the state which might be used for recreation and play. Our public school property is well equipped for many kinds of recreation. To use our present public buildings and parks and other city property involves not primarily the expenditure of money, but the conversion of public opinion and the establishment of social customs.

So far we have been content to devise means which by their nature are inadequate. A city of 40,000 regarded its problem of the older girls settled when it established an evening school accommodating 80 girls. Another city of 35,000 established a boys' club capable of holding 100 boys, and the citizens felt that they had provided adequate sources of exercise and recreation. These are actual cases. New York City has spent millions for playgrounds in Manhattan, but in 1906 the playgrounds could accommodate only about 7 per cent of the children below Fourteenth Street. We need to face the recreation problem fairly and deal with it adequately, not only for children but for adults as well.

The problem of the recreation of the adult is not identical with the problem of the play of children. There is a real difference also between play and recreation. The function of play in the life of the individual, and the function of recreation, are problems that must be solved before undertaking public provision for these needs. The boy who is playing football with intensity needs recreation as much as does the inventor who is working intensely at his invention. Play may be more exhausting than work, because one can play much harder than one can work. No one would dream of pushing a boy in school as hard as he pushes himself in a football game. If there is any difference of intensity between play and work, the difference is in favor of play. Play is the result of desire; for that reason it is often carried on with more vigor than is work.

Recreation is different in character. It consists, for the adult, in reversion to the simpler fundamental activities acquired during childhood. It means relaxation in contrast to the child's outlet of energy. The intense adult plays may be as exhausting as the intense plays of children. For the adult who is working strenuously in his business, it is not sufficient that he shall be strenuous in his play. He has another and quite different need, the need for recreation.

THE PLAY OF ADULTS

If we define play as doing that which we want to do, without reference primarily to any ulterior end, but simply for the joy of the process, then there are many activities of the adult in addition to his recreation which come in this category. The distinction is one of mental attitude, not of actual activities. The feeling of choice and desire is the determining element in play.

Mark Twain said in regard to the tasks of his life: "I have not done a day's work in my life. What I have done I have done because it has been play. If it had been work I should not have done it." Adrian Kirk, in an article entitled "Masters of their Craft," shows how this feeling toward work may animate men in widely different professions. A bus-driver, a motor-man, an engineer, a type-setter, may take the play attitude toward his tasks. "I'd rather run a car than eat," said the motor-man. "I've been offered charge of the stable, but I'd rather drive," was the statement of the cabman.

A series of letters from millionaires attempted to answer the question: "Why do men keep on making money when they have enough?" There were letters from Michael Cudahy, D. K. Pearsons, W. S. Kimball, and a number of others. Nearly all of these men spoke of "the fascination of the game." It was not the concrete result that they wanted; it was the process which attracted them—the opportunity to go on, to outplay, to outgeneral. They had long passed the mark they set for themselves. But to drop out of the game! A boy does not drop out of a game of football when he is fascinated by it. That is the attitude of play.

The term play is used popularly in many different senses. It is frequently contrasted with work and held to cover a series of activities which are highly enjoyable, but quite without utility or seriousness. Or it is confounded with recreation, and its usefulness is found solely as a means of relaxation and preparation for future work. As a result of this view the plays of children are excused on the ground that children are not yet able to do the serious tasks of the world, and may therefore be allowed to enjoy themselves without much loss. But play is not something less serious than work. It differs from what we may call work in mental attitude rather than in actual activity or output of energy. Play, in the scientific sense, the sense in which we shall use it, is the term we give to a series of activities as wide as the scope of human action, when those activities are performed not from external compulsion, but as an expression of the self, as the result of desire. In this sense the problem of play is the problem of a rich and free life; the problem of recreation is only one of its phases.

CHAPTER X

THE PLAY OF SUBNORMAL CHILDREN

THE first subnormal boy of whom I had charge was already in his teens, but he could not count to five. He showed no interest in anything that involved effort. He could run somewhat, but he did not like to run, for he considered it hard work. He seldom engaged in any form of exercise. If I took him by the hand and ran with him around the gymnasium track, he would follow like a dog trotting behind me, but he hated it. I told him that if he could keep count of the number of times we went around, we would run only five times, whereas if he did not keep count, we would run twice five. For the first time in his life that boy desired definite intellectual power. He struggled to count five, in order that he might not have to run more than that number of times. After a while he accomplished it, and within a week he could count up to twenty. His desire to learn to count called forth all the latent power that was in him. That boy later went to college.

PLAY OF SUBNORMAL CHILDREN

He possessed a good heredity and a good brain, but there was some defect of will and initiative that had to be overcome. After that initial experience he went forward rapidly.

This boy was an exceptional case. Results such as this cannot be expected in the case of all feeble-minded children. However, a study of the play of subnormal children, made by the teacher of a subnormal class in Springfield, Massachusetts, shows that lack of energy and initiative is one of the most marked characteristics of all the actions of feeble-minded children. She divided the children into low grade, middle grade, and high grade, and described them as follows:

I. *Low Grade.*—In visiting the playrooms of low-grade, feeble-minded children, the dominant impression is that of inactivity. One child among twenty-four has been seen aimlessly piling blocks on one another, one rocking a doll, the rest swaying back and forward, playing with their fingers or feet, looking at each other or staring out of the window.

II. In a somewhat higher grade more activity is seen. Blocks are arranged apparently according to some idea in the mind, dolls are dressed and undressed; there is some individualistic play with toys and dolls. When turned loose on a playground, some children show varied play activities, though the majority stand about or run with no apparent object. Occasionally a child is seen swinging and a few are digging in the sand.

III. The highest grade may be seen in groups about the playground. The casual observer may think that some interesting game is in progress, but, upon nearing the group, nothing of the kind will be discovered—simply aimless talking, waiting for an outside stimulus. One more active than the rest may be at the head of a little band whom he is leading as soldiers, but few join the ranks as they march about. A ball nine may be formed, but unless some normal person is present to stimulate and encourage, the game falls flat. Competitive sports seem to be enjoyed only under the direction of an attendant.

Spontaneity in play is a chief lack of feeble-minded children. The lower the grade, the less spontaneous is the play activity, and the more individualistic is the play, when, indeed, there is any play at all. The higher the grade, the greater are the indications of activity, but the play is still largely individualistic and non-competitive unless there is some outside stimulus.

These findings are corroborated by some observations recorded in a special class in a public school. These children would compare in ability with the middle and higher grades of the first set of observations.

I. *Low Grade.* These children have little activity when set free on the playground, other than an aimless running about. They may try to catch some one who is running, but they never succeed in having a group game of tag. They would not know who was "it." They never spin tops or play with

PLAY OF SUBNORMAL CHILDREN 131

marbles, though they may possess them. They never originate games. No girl in this class has failed to respond to the attraction of a doll, but the play is confined to dressing and undressing it, holding it, and walking with it. With blocks they make the very simplest forms, usually in imitation of some other child.

Limited power of co-ordination is shown by inability to catch a bean bag or ball, the forearms being used in the effort instead of the hands. When the ball is thrown up vertically, the arms come together *after* the ball has touched the floor. In every attempt to vary the exercise a tendency is shown to play according to the *old* directions, not the *new*.

Rosa, aged seven, when given a ball, was unable on entrance to follow directions, and for weeks simply rolled the ball ahead of her on the floor, running after it like a two-year-old child, although others about her were playing in many different ways. After some months she succeeded in bounding and catching it once out of five times. When given a wooden ping-pong bat, she was unable to use it with a ball.

II. *High Grade.*—All suggestions for original play come from this group. Occasionally a game of tag is organized, racing games are suggested, demands that "sides" be chosen. A few spin tops and play marbles, but the latter never as a contest.

Power of adaptation to new directions is much greater, as well as power to co-ordinate. One case was noted of bounding the ball and catching it in time to the rhyme, "I asked my mother for fifty cents to see the elephant jump the fence," etc. Complicated constructions are made with blocks.

Increase of mental activity is coexistent with increase of play activity.

We are not now considering the congenital idiots, nor the hopeless cases of feeble-mindedness, neither are we referring particularly to the cases of arrested development caused by adenoids, defective vision, or defective senses of any kind. Most of the work that has been done in the past has been with reference to the exceptionally low-grade idiot, whom it is impossible to educate to the standards of normal life. But such cases constitute only from one-half to two per cent of the school population, whereas there are from five to eight per cent of subnormal children who may be converted to usefulness by the establishment of right habits of muscular conduct, and by the stimulation of the will.

The plays of these subnormal children show, then, certain very marked differences from those of normal children. The most immediately noticeable fact is perhaps the absence of energy. There is less energy of endurance, less energy of each muscular contraction, less energy of effort. The feeble-minded are careless. They do not care whether they are "tagged" or not. They are not warmly enthusiastic about their play. This condition does not make for progress. The play is subnormal in almost all directions, both from the physical and the mental side.

Most of these children are deficient physically.

PLAY OF SUBNORMAL CHILDREN 133

The skin of many of them is clammy, showing a lack of circulation. They exhibit a marked inability to use any part of the body with skill. They have a characteristic shuffling gait, which is evidence of a lack of precise co-ordinations, and they are usually lacking in muscular power. But the most noticeable deficiency is that of will power. Their desire to sit still and do nothing is perhaps their most marked differentiation from normal children. They need an extraordinary stimulus of some kind, imitation or compulsion, to induce activity.

In the duration and variety of their plays, these subnormal children are also strikingly deficient. They make practically no progress from month to month and year to year. They may live to adult life in an institution, and unless they are taught to play other and more complex plays, they will do the same things over and over again.

Play is thus seen to be an indication of the capacity for growth. The play of the normal individual goes on to fresher and fresher interests, and when one thing is mastered, he puts that behind him for background and acquires something new. That means growth and power. This growth the feeble-minded lack. They are not only feeble in regard to intellectual pursuits, such as reading, writing and arithmetic. They are feeble when it comes to thinking of anything new to do in play. They do not acquire the higher forms of play developed by normal children. Competitive play needs to be taught, and team play seems almost completely beyond their capacity.

Subnormal children also differ from normal children in the place which tradition and imitation has in their plays. There are two factors which make play: the desire, or instinct, which gives the driving motive; and the tradition which decides what form the play shall take. Feeble-minded children lack not only the spontaneous impulse to play; they also possess to a very much lessened degree than the normal child the power of carrying social tradition. If feeble-minded children are taught some interesting games adapted to their development, and are then put with other children who have not been so taught, the children who know the games will not propagate them. Among normal children a good game spreads from child to child. But subnormal children must be taught individually and with great care.

The physical movements which adults make are imitated unconsciously by most children as soon as they reach the age for those move-

PLAY OF SUBNORMAL CHILDREN 135

ments. On the other hand, to teach a feeble-minded boy to use a hammer requires very minute pedagogical steps. To teach the feeble-minded girl to cut out a pattern, to use scissors, to follow a line, involves great patience and stages of teaching which the normal girl seems almost to omit entirely, so unconsciously does she pass through them. The power of imitation in subnormal children is very low.

Lack of spontaneous effort, of desire, of variety, and of the unconscious imitation by which normal children learn so many muscular co-ordinations—these seem to be the chief deficiencies of subnormal individuals, in play and in all other activities. The way of development, then, lies in the acquiring of these motor accomplishments. The treatment of the feeble-minded before the days of Seguin was primarily directed to the intelligence, and it failed. Seguin worked on the hand training of the idiot; he laid the foundation for all that has been done since. He taught the subnormal child the same muscular contractions that are made unconsciously by the normal child.

The use of rhythmical exercises has been found to be of great benefit in the education of subnormal children. In the Massachusetts Institute for the Feeble-minded, Doctor Fernald has utilized rhythm with reference to muscular labor. He says that if he can get boys to shovel or hammer, using heavy sledges, and with many working in unison, they will do several times as much work through the effect of rhythm as they would do if they were in a position which required them constantly to make a choice. They can thus develop the needed muscular co-ordinations more surely and with greater ease.

Physical education, especially through play, is the best means for the education of the feeble-minded. The first step is to create a desire to run, to throw, to stand up straight, to do something. This desire can be aroused more easily in connection with the oldest, most fundamental human reactions, than in any other way. The folk-dance is particularly effective in this direction, because of the rhythmic actions involved. Another good method of training is to give exercise combined with some game or story. A teacher who had blocks of wood on the floor told the children to step from one to the other for "if they missed one of the stepping-stones in the brook, they would get wet." In this way she succeeded in arousing interest and in teaching some of the fundamental co-ordinations necessary for further development.

I once had charge of a little feeble-minded girl

PLAY OF SUBNORMAL CHILDREN

whose attention I could not hold. Without attention, education is, of course, impossible. At last I hit upon the expedient of making her stand with one foot close in front of the other. Then if she did not give attention she would fall. From that time on she made progress. Physical education, given in connection with play, is the most direct method to this end.

There is a class of children who can by no means be classed as feeble-minded, but in whose play abnormal conditions of life have produced some of the same characteristics we have been discussing. These are the children in institutions. Miss Florence L. Lattimore has written of them:

> I have seen children at play in about one hundred institutions, and, beyond the use of toys, I have never seen any game but tag. Repeatedly I have been told by caretakers that "they like to stand around and watch each other." In photographing the so-called playground of one of these institutions, I tried to take a picture of the children at play; but they did not know how to pose for me, and they had never been taught even how to play tag. They just ran around and pushed one another.
> In one institution some fifty little boys are daily sent to a cement-floored basement at playtime. There is no supervision. The president of the institution told me that they did not seem to know what to do with themselves, and dug the putty from

138 A PHILOSOPHY OF PLAY

around every one of the panes of glass in the windows. They were reprimanded for this and told to *play*. Not knowing how, they scooped out little crescents of cement from the floor in a sort of pattern, and when they were reprimanded for this, they sat around in a kind of limp despair. The children tell me that they "don't like to play because of the bullies." In other words, competition is not fair in their undirected play, and the children who do not like free fights keep out of the playtime activities. I have known this to be true of institution after institution. The apparent contentment of these children, their lassitude and calm, is commonly mistaken for a satisfied play instinct. Close study of these little inmates reveals that lack of bodily tone, of motivation, and opportunity to learn to play are the chief factors in this group passivity.

This quotation is important as showing the subnormal state into which otherwise normal children may be thrown by lack of proper opportunity and traditions for play. The lack of motivation, of ability to carry on the higher forms of team play, are characteristic also of feeble-minded children. Miss Sadie American says of institution children: "It is absolutely necessary to inject into them, not only the desire to play, but the habit of play." She quotes Mr. Lowenstein of the Hebrew Orphan Asylum in New York as saying that while there is plenty of outdoor space for the children of that institu-

PLAY OF SUBNORMAL CHILDREN 139

tion, they stand about watching those who have already been taught and they have to be led into the play before they will indulge in it.

A model asylum visited by Miss Eugenie Macrum, of Pittsburg, revealed an identical condition. It was an invigorating winter afternoon, but not a child had been outdoors. The sisters felt too cold to leave the house and had taken it for granted that none of the children would care to go out. No child had the enterprise to propose an excursion into the open. The asylum grounds were large and situated in a beautiful neighborhood. A snowball fight would no doubt have been cheerfully permitted, but there was no one to take the initiative.

"Play expresses spiritual as well as physical exuberance," says Mrs. Harriet Hickox Heller, of the Douglas County Detention School, in Nebraska. "In the sick, exhausted, imbecile, abnormal child, play decreases in a suggestive ratio. In proportion as they are abnormal, these children seem to lose the power of exercising the self-expressing, creative play. Without the experience of play their chances of normal maturity are too meager to risk. They must be taught to play."

To some extent this same lack of spontaneity and play initiative is found in large numbers of city children. Miss American describes a game called "Long Branch" which some little girls were playing on a city sidewalk. It was a deadening occupation, consisting merely in seeing who could flip a stone farthest. "Those children should have been playing hop-scotch or prisoner's base; but the stimulus to such play had been destroyed through lack of use." Long lines of children used to stand in the play grounds of Chicago waiting for an opportunity to swing, without sufficient knowledge or initiative to invent any other amusement than the one which was already over-occupied. A clever play leader started a game and relieved the congestion.

The play of feeble-minded children is characterized by lack of initiative, of desire, of energy, of variety, of social tradition. These same deficiencies are making an appearance in some unlooked-for places. If it be true, as it has been stated, that many of the children of New York do not know how to play, it is a fact startlingly worth considering in connection with the relation which the play stimulus and play tradition sustain relative to normal development.

CHAPTER XI
PLAY PROGRESSION

A MOST attractive theory was put forward some years ago. It was called the "Culture-epoch" theory. It held that children went through the same epochs that are represented by the different tribes and nations in the development from savagery to civilized life. There was first the stage of migration and wandering, when the race lived in families and went from place to place; later there was the agricultural stage. It was maintained that these instinct feelings constitute great psychic zones through which the race passed and out of which it drew various lessons. Therefore, the individual also must go through zones of this kind, and school life should be adjusted accordingly. In the nomadic stage children should have the literature which developed in the nomadic age, and their art should be related to the kind of art developed then. Their interest in plants and animals should be centred in the plants and animals known by the race in that period; the history studied should be that of the nomadic stage.

Let us examine this theory in the light of observed sequences in children's spontaneous plays. When does the hunting instinct begin in the boy? The exact time has not been determined, but we know that a baby under two years of age enjoys running away and being pursued. He also enjoys trying to catch some one else. Nor can it be shown that the hunting instinct ever ceases. There is no age when men are too old to enjoy fishing. This does not mean that all men enjoy fishing, but if a man has enjoyed it as a boy, he does not lose interest in fishing while he is alive and well.

The other day I saw two men, one about forty and the other seventy-five years old, coming in from the river. They had a basket about ten inches long, seven inches high, and eight inches wide, in which they had brought their lunch and fishing-tackle. These men had been fishing all day. They had eaten their lunch and used up their bait, and had about fifty fish. These fifty fish did not weigh as much or take up as much space as the lunch and bait had taken. They had secured many fish too small to eat, and had spent a day in doing it. But they were happy. They were not too old to have the keenest enjoyment in fishing.

There is no need of going into an extended

PLAY PROGRESSION 143

discussion of the way in which the hunting feeling, in a modified form, enters into the competition of business and professional life. Most of the intensity of the business world is built on these old instincts of fighting and hunting. Men stay in business for the fascination of the game long after the main reason for working has disappeared. But leaving this out of account, and keeping to the simpler level of hunting as hunting, there is no definite age at which a man ceases to want to hunt. He may acquire new feelings which keep him from hunting, feelings of sympathy for the animals, but the hunting instinct never dies. He never becomes too old or loses the early interest. The hunting "epoch" extends from birth until death.

The shelter interest is equally permanent. Little children three years old enjoy playing house. This play corresponds to deep feelings within them. Boys and girls in their teens love their shacks in the woods and the little houses they have built in the yard, and the trees they have for their own. Young married people have the same feeling very strongly when they move into a new home, a permanent shelter which is theirs. Old married people with families experience these shelter feelings when they return to the old home. Grandparents have told me that to go back to the place of their childhood and to see their children and children's children around them arouses profound feelings of the shelter type. There is no shelter epoch except the epoch of human life.

There is no epoch in friendship. There are, indeed, times when friendship grows fastest. Middle life is somewhat of a fearsome period for one thing because new human relationships are established then with much greater difficulty than in the teens. The friends acquired during the twenties, who have kept together enough to share life's experiences, remain closer friends than most people who come together later in life. The friendship feeling does not come in one particular period and then go out of existence.

The same is true of other interests. The child who has loved dogs and cats, cows and chickens, horses and sheep and ducks does not lose this interest in mature years. The relationships to the natural world that come through these associations do not die. The love of plants and the interest in gardens are not confined to a single epoch. Those whose hearts have been thrilled by the beauties of the woods, the lights and the shadows, the flash of the sun on the water, do not pass out of this stage.

PLAY PROGRESSION

There may be times when the soul can respond more vividly than at other times, but there is no epoch in the love of nature.

A child does not go through an "Indian stage." I have seen boys play Indian with great intensity. They had their tepees and bows and arrows, their councils and Indian fights. But the next hour they might be playing policeman, or fire-engine, using a wholly different set of interests, those of a culture period a thousand years removed from their first play. No theory could well have been elaborated that was farther from the observed facts of human life than the culture-epoch theory. This does not mean that there is no order in physical, mental, moral, and social development. The more complicated must always be built on the simple. But to put these instincts in strata and say: "This is the time for the hunting instinct and then that goes out; this is the time for the property instinct and then that goes out"—is false from all we know of children's plays.

Child nature has no culture epochs of this kind. Interests in different plays come, sometimes together, sometimes one ahead, sometimes the other ahead. There is no absolute order in the eruption of these great passionate lifelong feelings. Under the stimulus of the hunting feeling a little boy will run about; under the stimulus of the same feeling he will play tag, and the tag will grow more complicated as he grows older. Later he will play baseball from the same impulse, and still later he may go into scientific research. The feeling which dominates and guides his life furnishes a constant spring of motive, taking on new forms of activity with ever-increasing complexity.

There is indeed a play progression related not to the acquisition of new fundamental instincts, but to the physical and mental development of the individual. A baby does not make the same complicated movements that a boy of ten makes. There is a close relation between the particular games in which the various instincts express themselves and the development of the heart, lungs, muscles, and especially of the nervous system. Boys do not play running games before the heart has reached a certain balance. Games demanding endurance do not normally occur before the pubertal development of the heart and arteries has occurred. There is a relation from infancy to adult life between the games that are played and the part of the individual that is growing.

At about the age of seven or eight the boy wants to play marbles. He does not say: "My

PLAY PROGRESSION 147

motor areas are now ripening and I will help them in their development by using my fingers." But that is precisely what he is doing without knowing it. The same thing is true of other games. They develop in successive years in complexity, in intensity, in rapidity. They are suited to the growing needs of the individual. The chart entitled "Anglo-Saxon Play"[1] will serve for a general outline of play progression. Nothing exact is indicated by this diagram. There is no real division between children of six and those of seven, or between children of thirteen and fourteen. Moreover, there are always individual variations. But on the whole there is a great distinction between the plays that are most prominent between birth and the age of seven, and those prominent between the years of seven and twelve. There is a similar distinction with reference to the games played in the teens. The difference is chiefly one of emphasis; some boys and girls never reach the third stage, some never pass beyond the first. Yet there is a general progression; the later games are based from the necessity of the case upon the earlier. A boy cannot jump before he has learned to walk; he cannot throw until he has learned to drop objects and pick them up. As children be-

[1] See page 154.

come more skillful in the use of certain muscle combinations, they go on to more complex plays. The direction of the curved lines in the chart indicates that these interests of life are permanent. At any age all the previous interests still survive. Other more complex activities come into the child's life and push the elementary plays into the background; later still larger interests are built upon the earlier, with more complex ethical and social relations. But when we take time for the earlier activities, we still discover joy in doing them. I presume that it is still interesting to us to sit on a beach and let the fine sand trickle through our fingers, to make little piles of it, to dig gardens and walks of sand. We do not do it as often as we did when we were children, for more interesting matters have claimed our attention. We have more capacity for work and pleasure than we had then; we revert to these simple pleasures only in times of fatigue when we wish to rest. Then we lay aside the more recently developed, more exhausting activities, because they are more complex and utilize more of our entire personality.

The first group of plays indicated in the chart is individualistic. These plays relate to control of the body. The child learns to use his hands, to run, to balance himself, to throw, to jump. The complex arm movements of later games are built on these earlier attainments. There is a tremendous joy in these early attainments. I remember watching a little boy of five years learning to throw. He showed great excitement as he changed from putting, which is the throw of children and most women, to the man's throw, in which the weight of the whole body goes into the movement. He had accomplished a new thing. A great part of the joy of early childhood is related to this progressive mastery of self and of the environment.

From self-mastery the boy goes on to competition with others. Little children do not care to compete, and should never be stimulated by competition. They have not learned self-mastery and self-control. Unfair play is partly traceable to engaging in competition before self-control has been attained. With self-mastery comes the desire to master others, to compete in running, at marbles, at tag, in swimming. The intensity with which boys pursue the running, jumping, throwing, striking games, such as "Duck on the rock" and "One old cat," indicates the power of the instinct feelings that hold them. There is nothing in the games themselves to account for their tremendous grip. A boy will learn to throw in "One old cat" as he never learns to throw for the pure joy of throwing. He gains a new kind of self-mastery through this competition. His chief object, however, is to master the other boy.

In the third group, the elements of self-mastery and competition still remain, but something new is added, team loyalty. Many boys never reach the third stage. The essence of these games is self-sacrifice for the group, which is the great masculine source of altruism. The boy who hustles for himself and not for his gang is the boy who cannot play these games. He is also the boy who does not develop the wider loyalty of manhood. A boy begins by being loyal to one or two friends, then to a dozen, then to his school, and finally to his community.

There are other relations between plays besides that of progression from the simple to the complex. No one who has noticed plays at all has failed to observe the seasonal rotation of games. The advent of spring is more surely marked by the games of marbles played on the street than by the coming of bluebirds and robins. The birds may fail, for there may be a late spring. But I have seen marbles played in the snow in Springfield, because it was marble

PLAY PROGRESSION

time. The season had come, even if the snow had not gone.

All over the world the plays of children rotate with great regularity. This is more true in a stable community than in a new town. In an old English village, where people are living as they have lived for generations, the plays come around with perfect precision. In Japan the sequence of plays is most regular. Even in our own communities the venders of implements for children's play know what stock to order for every season. I secured records of the plays of 11,000 children in a western city at one time, and classified them. The record showed that while there are many plays engaged in at random, the larger games are seasonal. Tag, hide-and-seek, marbles, and ball are among these games. Interest in dolls does not rotate, but the things which are done with dolls rotate.

This rotation of plays is not the same in any two cities or countries I have studied. It is true that in the main kites are flown during the time of the year in which there is most wind, and marbles are usually played when the ground is suitable. But if there are several periods of high wind, kites will be flown in only one of them, and this particular time will vary in different communities. Except for those plays which are wholly dependent on the weather, as skating, sliding downhill or snowballing, games may come at different times of the year in different cities, but in the same city the rotation is a fixed one.

This seems to show that it is not the order of rotation which is significant, but the fact of rotation. There is not the same order of games in New York, Chicago, and Tokio, but there is the same fact of a seasonal change. One play does not of itself lead into another play, or the order of rotation would be stable. This fact that one play comes to a natural conclusion, and that there is then a demand for another play—just what other play is not universally determined—bears an interesting relation to growth.

Growth proceeds by pulses, not in a straight line. We do not grow in height a little every day until our full stature is secured. We grow for certain weeks and then there will be weeks in which we do not grow in height, but rather in breadth. We tend to grow in height in the spring, and in weight in the fall. Even during successive years there is no uniformity of growth. In certain years, perhaps from nine to eleven or twelve, the child will grow only about an inch a year; and then in a succeeding year he may add three, four, five, or six inches to his stature.

PLAY PROGRESSION

Growth in the ability to acquire a language is in pulses. I have the records of the words used by all of my own children up to the age of two. In two or three days the child may learn fifteen to twenty new words, and then for a whole month he may not learn any more. He may even forget the words he has learned. There are pulses in vital power and in every form of enthusiasm. This is the meaning of the seasonal rotation of plays.

These pulses do not coincide in all individuals. If I should measure the growth in height of 11,000 children up to the age of twelve years and take an average, I should have a steady curve. But no child grows by a curve of that kind. It is the average, but it is false to every individual child that contributes to that average. The length and appearance of the pulses of interest vary with different ages and different individuals.

There is, then, a progression in play, from simple to complex co-ordinations. Certain kinds of play precede others. The great fundamental instincts never cease, but the form of their expression varies. There is also a seasonal rotation in plays corresponding to the growth of the individual, which is always by pulses. The play progression has physical, mental, and moral relations to the development of the individual.

CHART OF ANGLO-SAXON PLAY[1]

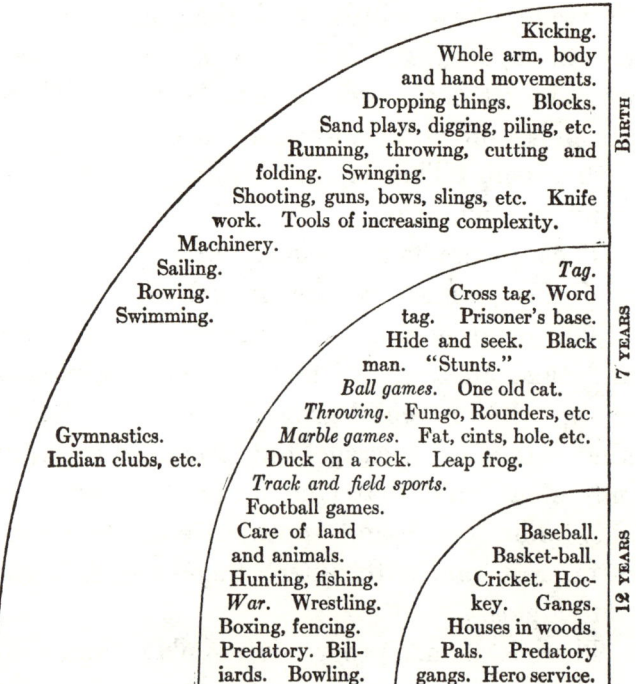

[1] Pedagogical Seminary, 1899, vi, 137.

CHAPTER XII

PLAY AND PHYSICAL GROWTH

ONE of the most evident characteristics of a new-born baby is its movements—the motions of its hands, face, legs, arms, feet, mouth, eyebrows. Immediately after birth, the child begins to make separate finger movements, but he is not able to do this with conscious direction for several years. During the time when he is coming into this conscious control, the child's chief interest is related definitely to his movements. To watch the plays of children with reference to their physical development is a fascinating process. Each period in life is marked by a new interest, which corresponds exactly to the neuro-muscular development of that period. Thus the interests of children are of the greatest significance, not because they please the children, but because they correspond to vital processes going on in the child's body, mind, and character.

The amount of physical exercise which the average child obtains through his ordinary play when free to move about and conduct himself

156   A PHILOSOPHY OF PLAY

as he pleases, is inconceivable to the adult until he takes the trouble to make an actual record of the number of movements performed by some child in the space of half an hour. I have obtained a number of records of this kind. The following is the account of the movements of a boy of four during one hour.

8:00 A. M. TO 9:00 A. M.

Breakfast. Raised arm from plate to mouth 50 times. Jumped down from chair. Lifted curtains. Took out blocks and cards. Stood up straight; repeated 8 times. Came down on his knees. Set cards upon window-sill (in crack between window and sill). Ran across with card. Knees in chair and whirled around. Stooped and picked up a card. Ran with it across the room; repeated 15 times. Turned around and swung his arm. Went upstairs to third story with hands in pockets. Walked around, raised his arm to touch things on table. Went down-stairs with considerable enthusiasm. Skipped across the hall. Stooped, picked up leggins. Went up-stairs. Went down-stairs. Scuffed around swinging his arms (not angry, just steam working off). Ran up-stairs. Sat down at table and twirled a box around. Lay down on couch. Ran across hall and part way down-stairs. Lay down flat on landing. Got up. Stooped half-way. Ran across room. Sat down on floor to put on shoe. Buttoned one shoe. Lay on couch swinging feet in air. Hanging from hands and feet between two articles of furniture. Got on head of couch and slid down on his abdomen. Pulled on other shoe. Rolled to sitting posture on the floor. Sat on couch. Slid to floor again. Lay with feet up, looking at shadows cast by his performance. Ran across hall and down-stairs and opened door. Climbed into chair, swung his feet.

PLAY AND PHYSICAL GROWTH 157

If in that exercise all the body movements could have been put together, and all the arm flexions together, it would have been exceedingly fatiguing. The way in which the child combines a variety of movements when he is playing freely gives the greatest amount of exercise with the least amount of fatigue. He is in constant motion, but the motion is always changing. This is in sharp contrast to the methods employed in our school gymnastics. There all the motions of one kind are performed in rapid succession; no method is more fatiguing than this. Moreover, the new neuro-muscular adjustments, which are acquired even more surely during rest following action than during action itself, are obtained much more readily through the method of play than through that of the gymnasium.

Here is a record of the muscular movements of a boy two and a half years old—the exercise taken in an ordinary day, without suggestion or stimulation.

8:00 A. M.

Child was sitting down 15 minutes, playing (arm movements only). He stood up, sat down in new position, 16 arm movements, 4 bendings from waist. Stood up, stooped twice picking up toys. Sat down, 3 arm movements, 2 bendings; 4 arm movements, 1 bending. Stood up, stooped over. Sat down, 3 arm movements, 1 bending,

3 arm movements. Threw ball across the room. Stood up, 3 arm movements. Walked few steps, 6 arm movements. Walked 8 steps, 2 arm movements. Picked up block, sat down, 2 arm movements, 1 bending. Stood up, 1 bending, 2 arm movements. Sat down, 1 bending, 6 arm movements, 1 bending. Stood up, walked 10 steps. Stooped, walked back 10 steps, 3 arm movements. Walked 2 steps, stooped, 2 arm movements, 1 bending. Walked 3 steps, stooped, 2 arm movements. Walked 6 steps, stooped, 2 arm movements. Sat down, 3 arm movements, 1 bending, 1 arm movement. Threw block, 1 arm movement, 1 bending, 4 arm movements, 1 bending, 2 arm movements, 1 bending, 1 arm movement, 1 bending, 4 arm movements, 2 bendings, 1 arm movement, 4 leg movements. Stood up, 1 arm movement. Walked 3 steps, 1 bending, 3 arm movements; walked 5 steps, stooped, 2 arm movements. Walked 5 steps, stooped, 4 arm movements. Walked across the room, 3 arm movements. Walked across room twice, 2 arm movements. Walked across the room again, 6 arm movements. Stooped, 5 arm movements, 3 leg movements. Walked 6 steps, 2 arm movements.

Climbed on mother's lap and off again. Walked several steps, stooped, picked up toy. Walked back, 2 arm movements. Leaned against mother, swaying back and forth. Walked a few steps, stood rocking from side to side 14 times. Sat down; 7 arm movements, 3 leg movements, 4 bendings. Stood up. Walked 7 steps, 4 arm movements. Ran across room and back, swinging one arm. Stooped. Took 6 steps, 1 arm movement, 4 steps, 8 arm movements. Ran across room and back, 1 arm movement. Sat on table, 4 arm movements, 4 leg movements, 1 bending, 1 arm movement. 1 bending, 1 arm movement, 4 leg movements, 2 arm movements, 1 bending, 1 arm movement, 1 leg movement, 3 arm movements, 1 bending, 2 arm movements, 1 bending, 4 arm movements, 1 bending, 7 arm movements, 1 leg movement, 1 bending, 5 arm movements, 2 leg movements, 3 arm movements, 2 bend-

PLAY AND PHYSICAL GROWTH 159

ings, 5 arm movements, 2 bendings, 3 arm movements 3 leg movements.

Sat on mother's lap, 11 arm movements, 1 bending, 2 arm movements, 1 bending, 1 arm movement, 1 bending, 1 arm movement. Got down on floor. Walked across room 4 times, 3 arm movements. Sat down, 3 arm movements. Stood up. Walked 5 steps, crouched down 5 times. Picked up blocks and threw them across the room. Walked 8 steps. Swayed 6 times, 10 steps, crouched down. Stood up, 4 steps, 2 arm movements. Ran across room and back, 1 arm movement. Crawled over mother's lap as she sat on the floor; 3 steps, 2 arm movements. Ran across room and back, 2 arm movements. Ran across room, stooped. Came back, 4 arm movements, 7 steps, 3 arm movements. 1 bending, 2 arm movements. Crossed room, came back, 6 arm movements. Ran length of two rooms twice. Sat down, playing with blocks, 9 arm movements. Stood up, 4 steps. Picked up block. Walked back. Sat down, 4 arm movements, 1 arm movement, 1 bending, 2 bendings. Stood up, took 30 steps. Picked up blocks. Sat down, 1 bending, 4 arm movements, 1 bending, 2 arm movements, 1 bending. Stood up. Took 5 steps. Swayed back and forth. Ran across two rooms and back, 1 arm movement. Walked across room, pulling little wagon. Came back length of two rooms, 6 times, swinging arms.

Sat down, spinning little wheel, 18 arm movements. Stood up. Walked 13 steps, 11 arm movements. Walked length of two rooms, 9 arm movements. Walked length of two rooms and back, 5 arm movements. Took a book, turning over the pages, 4 arm movements. Walked across room. Ran across two rooms. Sat down, swinging arm 17 times. Stood up, 3 arm movements. Walked across room and back. Sat down, 2 arm movements. Climbed on lap, down again. Walked length of two rooms and back. Walked length of two rooms and back. Ran across room twice. Ran across room, 3 arm movements, 1 bending. Ran across two rooms, 2 arm movements. Ran across two rooms, 3 arm movements. For next ten minutes was walking or running about, without sitting down or doing anything in particular. For 10 minutes he sat on table, using only arm movements. Then he climbed flight of 14 steps. Was put to bed for a nap. Took 45 minutes to go to sleep. Half that time he was rolling or creeping over the bed. Slept two hours. Woke and had dinner. This took 25 minutes, during which time only arm movements were used. Sat on floor for 27 minutes, Turk-fashion, using arm movements and bendings from waist (about one arm movement in 3 seconds). Then he climbed flight of stairs again, was brought down and dressed to go out. This took 10 minutes and all that time he was squirming. (No other word will express it.)

Went out for 1½ hours. For ½ hour of this time he was visiting at another home, and was walking and running about the whole time. As soon as he returned home, he sat on the floor, playing with blocks, all arm movements, except an occasional leg movement in changing position. Stood up, swaying from side to side. Walked across room. Picked up 20 blocks, stooping for each one and placing it on the sofa 3 steps away. Piled them above his head, reaching as high as he could. Walked half across the room, pulled a chair away from the table and pushed it back. Pushed another five feet. Walked around it, then around the room. Picked up 2 blocks and then threw them down. Walked about 4 feet to a chair and rocked it 12 or 13 times. Ran the length of room, knelt down, sat down, building up blocks. Stood up. Ran length of room and to a chair, played with toys on it, using arm movements. Ran across room and back. Picked up one toy, carrying it into next room. Repeated this twice. Walked around large table. Walked length of two rooms 3 times. Walked around in a circle. Leaned against mother, swinging back and forth 3 times. Walked twice around mother, stooped 3 times to pick up blocks, rolling

PLAY AND PHYSICAL GROWTH 161

them down inclined plane. Picked up 10 more, stooped each time, and threw them as far as he could. Walked 7 steps. Picked up 8 blocks, throwing them down. Walked across room 3 times, picking up a block each time. Walked across room. Picked up 2 blocks. Walked back, laid them in box. Repeated this 4 times. Climbed on lap and off. Put hands together and swayed up and down 3 times. Climbed on lap and down again. Walked length of room 6 times.

Sat down. Stood up. Walked across room twice. Took blocks, 2 at a time, from sofa and threw them on the floor. Sat down. Stood up. Walked across room. Lay on his back for 2 minutes, kicking and rolling over. Sat on table 18 minutes; there were few leg movements during this time, but arm movements and bendings or swayings from his hips were continuous. Sat on lap 7 minutes, arm movements only. Got down on floor, ran around table, rocked large chair back and forth 17 times. Sat down. Stood up. Sat down. Stood up. Put head on lap as mother sat on floor, making an arch of his body. Sat down. Stood up. Walked across room. Walked about 4 minutes. Sat down, playing with blocks for 6 minutes (all arm and hip movements). Stood up and piled up some blocks, stooping 6 times. Stooped 6 times, lifting lid off box and letting it fall again. Ran around room. Picked up toy horn and blew it 4 times. Climbed on lap. Slid down. Played with doll 1 minute. Walked 6 steps. Picked up box, put block in and shook box until block fell out. Did this twice. Ran across room 15 times. Ran across room 4 times. Ran around room twice, then across twice. Picked up ball and threw it. Did same with another toy. Walked a few steps. Picked up 3 toys and set them on the floor. Sat down. Stood up. Walked to corner and picked up several things. Walked back. Sat down for 1 minute. Walked to bookcase twice (10 steps each way). Pulled out 4 books and put them back. Sat down. Played with toys 2 minutes.

At supper (15 minutes), arm movements only. Was

put to bed. For an hour was hardly still a minute, creeping and rolling about, sitting up and throwing himself back on mattress.

The length and width of each room was about 15 feet. Usually in crossing room, the child went only 12 feet of the length or width of the room. In going around the room he went 21 feet.

These are ordinary, not extraordinary, examples of the physical exercise taken by the average child in his play. We need to have brought to our remembrance the amount and kind of movements that children undertake freely, in order to realize how inadequate are the usual school gymnastics of fifteen to twenty minutes per day in giving the kind of exercise that the organism needs for development.

The progression of plays from one year to the next as the individual grows in maturity coincides with and helps to develop the entire muscular and nervous systems. The games played at twelve involve more muscular power than those played at seven. This can be clearly seen in the chart of Anglo-Saxon play. Not every game involves more muscular power than the one preceding it; some, marbles, for instance, require little muscular power. But in general a distinct progression can be noticed. Football, basket-ball, cricket, hockey, shinney, polo demand more physical strength than the baby or the little boy possesses.

PLAY AND PHYSICAL GROWTH

There is also a progression in speed. Notice the demand for speed in baseball, basket-ball, football, cricket, or lacrosse. These games all require instant response. Consider, for instance, the length of time that the baseball batter has to decide whether he will hit the ball or not, after it leaves the pitcher's hand. The ball must go about one-third or one-half the distance, between twenty or thirty feet, before the man can begin to decide. He must judge the curve of the ball and the speed and direction it will have when it reaches him. He must send out stimuli to the muscles that control the balancing of his body; as he strikes, he must bend forward and then run. He must adjust the knees, the back, and the pelvis. The ball is going at the rate of almost sixty feet in a second. It will reach the space where he must do his batting in less than a second. Compare the speed and precision demanded of the player with the muscular adjustment of the baby. Compare it even with that demanded in the games of the small boy, like "One old cat," which does not require instantaneous reaction. The difference in speed makes baseball a different game.

There is also growth in the amount of endurance demanded in play. One of the interesting facts in those records of the movements of small children is the brief length of time given to any particular activity. A baby six months old will go over all his plays several times a day if he has the opportunity, and he will play the same plays the next day, each one of them a little at a time. To keep a baby playing at the same thing for two or three hours is foolish and cruel, but to let a man play three minutes four times a day is just as foolish. The man has developed power, and growth of power means absorption for long periods of time.

The pulses of interest observed in the seasonal rotation of plays increase in length with growth. Early in the teens three months is about the length of consecutive interest and absorbing effort. Frequently it is less than that time and a change is demanded sooner. As he grows older the things which interest a boy remain of interest for a longer period. A pulse of interest in electricity may last for two or three years. The play interests differ in no fundamental respect from these other interests expressed in art, literature, and some work. Formerly I was disturbed by the fact that after about three months' work of a particular kind I was no longer intensely interested in the task. But I discovered that periods of recurring interest always come to unfinished jobs. The forcing of original, vital

PLAY AND PHYSICAL GROWTH 165

work beyond the period of interest is a great mistake. It tends toward the killing of fertility. That is the lesson of the recurrence of plays.

Enormous growth in the complexity of coordinations is also shown in the play progression. A small baby that cannot yet sit up learns first to hold its head, then to use its back. After a while it learns to take hold of objects, and finally follows the intensely interesting operation of learning how to throw. Very early it discovers its mouth, and learns to carry the hand to the mouth. It acquires conscious control of the hands. I remember the first time a baby of mine acquired the ability to hold and drop objects. The child was in a high chair and had a silver spoon on the tray. She took the spoon and dropped it to the floor. I picked it up and put it back on the tray; the baby dropped it again. The baby did this seventy-nine times without stopping; she was learning about falling things. After that she experimented similarly for a time with everything she could lay hands on. But before long she passed on to other activities. Learning to use a knife and fork is an achievement built on previous attainments. The stability, the power, the speed, the complexity of the later plays are built on the earlier ones.

Play reflects the muscular co-ordinations of the child at the time; it also assists in developing them.

Far more important for the child's best growth than any muscular development, or than any increase in strength, speed and complexity of movements, is vitality. In this all-around toning up of the physical system, play has one of its greatest contributions to make to our modern society. We have not yet learned how to obtain vitality from city living. City stock tends all the time to dwindle in resistance and recuperative power. In past generations it has had to be replenished by a constant inflow of strong country stock; and the conditions which have made that necessary in the past are even more in evidence to-day. Our industrial life lacks balance; it gives no roundness of development.

Everything conspires to bring the city-born child upon the stage of life with an oversensitive nervous system and an undertoned physique. This is an entirely logical result of city conditions as they now are. No amount of medical protection, of sanitary legislation, can make good this depletion of vitality. It can only be remedied by providing for the inhabitants of the city, most of all during their years of growth,

PLAY AND PHYSICAL GROWTH 167

the opportunities of all-around physical development such as have heretofore been found only outside its bounds. The city child needs a muscular system built up along the broad general lines of an unspecialized life, the sort of life his ancestors have known; and since this is not provided naturally in the midst of the artificiality of the city, it must be provided artificially.

We have begun to recognize the importance of muscles in the normal growth of personality. The nervous system and the muscular system are so vitally interrelated in the carrying on of all life's central activities, that to educate the former without at the same time making provision for the latter is fools' economy. All the most characteristic strains of modern civilization fall upon the nervous system. Yet it is the latest system of the body, biologically speaking, to reach its full complexity of development; and it is the part most easily shattered. The city forces the nervous system, like a plant in a greenhouse forced into flower before its natural time; and if an equilibrium is not in some way re-established, the undue pressure upon the functions least able to endure strain is likely to bring disaster. A tower needs foundation.

The demands of a city child's daily programme develop his physique only in partial and one-sided ways. He has no trees to climb, no swimming-hole to duck into, no garden to hoe, no wood to saw. He has no space available for playing the big all-around games, such as baseball and hockey. His hand may acquire skill in the manipulation of delicate things, his senses become precociously sharpened, his wits quickened and refined; but his body does not get its dues.

Out of 78,401 public school children examined in one year in New York City, 58,259 were found to be in need of medical attention. That does not speak very hopefully for the physical calibre of the next generation. And if the next generation is to fail us, our schools costing millions of dollars a year have no object. These schools look only toward the future; they are carried forward on the assumption that there is to be a generation more capable and a future richer than the past.

The routine physical training of the school will not help us much in this particular situation. The aim of this feature of our curriculum is to correct certain evils that necessarily result from the special conditions of the schoolroom—the bent back, the eye-strain, the shallow breathing, the mental fatigue. But schoolroom gymnastics can hardly reach farther than that aim.

PLAY AND PHYSICAL GROWTH 169

Even at their best they are hopelessly far from meeting the deeper physical needs of the child, needs which reach so far into the child's inner constitution that it would be quite as appropriate to call them spiritual needs. For from their very nature, school gymnastics must be formal, almost mechanical, giving little scope to the imagination, and appealing but slightly to the child's hungry instincts.

In order then to supply our city children with the opportunity for healthy, spontaneous, free growth from within, we must give them a chance to play. Play is nature's preparation for the business of later life. It finds its roots in the remote past when man lived by hunting and climbing and fighting; it looks forward to the time when each boy and girl must shoulder responsibilities—the care of the home, the conflicts of business and of politics. It sums up and it anticipates. It is life itself in miniature —not the narrow specialized life of the mechanic, salesman, clothes finisher, or accountant, but the broad, simple, diversified life of a more primitive humanity.

Play is the only equivalent that can replace the inheritance which the child has lost. It is the whole of the child that is called into action here: muscle, imagination, and moral force.

The response to these varied demands upon him is made eagerly, passionately, without any thought of obedience to authority. Play makes an instinctive appeal to every child.

We are learning that we have not paid all our debt to the future when we have established for our children protection against disease and given them the usual school education. Equally imperative is it that we should provide for the development from within of vitality and power of resistance. Healthy play does that, and it does even more; it stimulates and co-ordinates the growth of the entire muscular and nervous systems, in strength, in complexity and speed of adjustment, in endurance; and it accomplishes these results in the only way that is finally effective—the way of joyous self-expression.

CHAPTER XIII
PLAY AND EDUCATION

THE spontaneous development of the child's interests as shown in play varies in many particulars from the consciously directed development given by our modern type of education. Take, for instance, the interest shown by the high school or college boy in football. If he is a healthy, normal boy, during the football season he is interested in that game to the exclusion of almost everything else. If he sits down to study, ideas of football keep crowding in. He will dream football. He will lose his self-consciousness completely in the consciousness of the team on which he plays. He will go to bed thinking how to make a certain play, and he will sit in school working out plans for accomplishing certain moves in the game. That part of his mind concerned with football grows tremendously—out of all proportion to the actual amount of time spent on the subject. Then the interest in football drops, and in the spring comes baseball. Baseball now becomes his major interest and colors all his thoughts.

172 A PHILOSOPHY OF PLAY

It is not merely a question of an interest in physical activity overshadowing an intellectual interest. There is a principle here which may be used to great advantage in intellectual work as well. At about the age of eleven one of my daughters became much interested in birds. She was led to make a careful study of the birds in the neighborhood of our home; books treating of them were procured for her. She worked out much information from an encyclopædia. She accomplished surprising results which were out of proportion to the small amount of time actually spent on the subject. A father read to his daughter, who had barely reached the age when she could read herself, an interesting child's book on astronomy. She became greatly interested, and her father furnished her with the necessary books on astronomy. The child went through several heavy volumes before that pulse of interest was exhausted, although she had to use a dictionary with almost as much frequency as if she were studying a foreign language. As a special favor she was allowed on certain nights to sit up late enough to see the stars. She obtained a map of the sky and puzzled out constellation after constellation. Then her interest stopped rather suddenly and was never again revived with equal strength. How-

PLAY AND EDUCATION 173

ever, in that short time she had acquired a knowledge of astronomy of some extent and of much greater permanency than anything she learned in school that year.

A high school boy became interested in tracing out his genealogy. Both his father's and his mother's lines were peculiarly rich in illustrious ancestors. His interest lasted for two years. During that time he acquired such minute knowledge of detailed history, running back to the Middle Ages, that on two occasions he was asked to lecture to a university class on the social customs, family relations, and intimate personal history of certain epochs. He pushed certain lines of genealogy farther back than any one else had carried them, and could speak with such authority that he was asked to give his results for publication. He filled his rooms with coats-of-arms painted by himself, and in one year his Christmas presents to his friends consisted almost entirely of these. Then his interest dropped, and he went on to other activities.

These are merely extreme examples of what frequently happens in connection with the intellectual interests of boys and girls. A boy who becomes filled with a desire to find out about electricity, who is given a shop room and allowed to make bells, telegraph connections, and various appliances, obtains a technical knowledge of the subject which is far more extended and permanent than any which the school system of education has yet succeeded in giving its pupils.

Nor can it be claimed that the knowledge thus gained and the mental development secured pass with the pulse of interest. Let any one of us become immersed in a subject, think in it, and live in it, and then stop for a while. When next he approaches the subject, he will find that he has greater power and skill than before. A man who practised throwing balls kept a record of his increase in skill. When he had practised for six months, he stopped for six months. Then when he tried again, in his first three or four trials he did better than he had done at the end of six months' practice.

That is the way the successful work of the world is done, by pulses of interest, followed by periods of relative inactivity with reference to that interest. The great artistic feats of the world have been performed by people who work in that way. The great geniuses have contributed their work chiefly in periods of intense application followed by periods of relative quiet.

We have not made extensive application of this observation to our system of school instruction. If there are twenty subjects to be mastered, we divide the time into twenty equal parts and give equal time and emphasis to each. The results may be seen in extreme form in the following instance. A girl came to Pratt Institute and applied for advanced standing in geometry. The course there covered five recitations a week. She said that she had studied geometry for two years. "You must have covered much more work than we have," I said. "What book did you use?" She did not remember the name of the book. She could not remember one of the propositions, formulæ, or original problems. It appeared that she had studied geometry for two years, twenty minutes a week. Thus each period of interest was so far removed from the next that there was no cumulative effect. All the enthusiasm had been taken out of the subject by dabbling in it. It was like learning to play the piano or to swing Indian clubs by spending twenty minutes a week on practice.

The play curriculum gives us a most valuable suggestion here. The play curriculum of children beyond the age of babyhood does not have its subjects divided equally with all the plays pursued a little every day. It has a major and one or two minors. The little child has indeed shorter pulses of interest; he goes the rounds of his plays every day, and a little later in life every few days. But a boy or girl of eight, ten, or twelve years goes the round only once or twice a year. In the teens the pulse of interest may last one, two, or three years. These facts would seem to have very important implications for education. At present our school curriculum is divided, not pedagogically nor psychologically, but logically. Life interests are not so divided. The division of subjects in the school bears no resemblance to the spontaneous activities either of play or of life. Hence it tends toward fatigue and loss of efficiency.

In play, the new games are related to new dawning abilities. We find the boy wanting to make machinery and the girl to make the smaller articles of the household during the years when the finger muscles and the nerve centres controlling them are ripening. We should not change this order. We waste time and effort if we attempt to go counter to it. Some teachers of gymnastics try to get minute co-ordinations from children of an age when they are and should be totally incompetent to give such co-ordinations. Much effort is spent, and the child does not succeed. I once determined that my children should learn to swim at an early age. Be-

PLAY AND EDUCATION 177

fore they could learn to walk I put water in the bathtub, adding a little more every day, and tried to teach them to swim. I wasted many hours of my own time and my children's, and they did not learn to swim. At about the age of eight, they learned very easily, almost spontaneously. The reason for this may be that in the early years of life the head is large in proportion to the body, and that as the child grows older the proportions change. Whatever the theory, the fact remains that between eight and ten years of age, children learn to swim with ease. It is quite futile to try to teach children at one age what they will learn of themselves with great delight and rapidity a few years later.

The chief forces in play are instinct and tradition. Plays at various ages are based upon fundamental instinct feelings. They derive their interest for the child from the fact that they give him an opportunity for self-expression. He does not merely go through the activities of play; he chooses to go through them. Self-expression is in itself pleasurable; it is also in itself educational. There is no reason why the subjects of the school curriculum should not also be so adapted to the dawning abilities of the child as to call forth his free choice. An interest pursued from choice has much more educational value, both in the extent and permanency of knowledge gained, than has any subject to which the child is driven.

There is, however, a force other than mere instinct feeling which guides the choice of the child in play. Play traditions furnish the form in which the instinct feeling finds expression. One child in a group does not play marbles while another plays ball, and still another engages in a different game. Similarly, it would not be necessary in the schoolroom, in order that every child might have free self-expression, to have each study a different subject. What is necessary is to provide for strong pulses of interest in subjects related to the actual abilities of the child. The group requirements may quite easily furnish the actual social form which the subjects will take, and will provide for many children studying the same subject at the same time.

The reason for the great amount of truancy and vagabondage during the school age is to be found in the permanency of a wholesome juvenile nature, which has been suddenly plunged into an environment entirely out of joint with its instinct feelings. The remedy lies, not in a fruitless attempt to change the nature of children, or to turn back the wheels of a movement which has changed their environment, but in an

PLAY AND EDUCATION 179

intelligent constructive effort to adapt the new environment to the children's needs. The needs which are no longer provided for at home and which are most definitely related to idleness and vagabondage are those connected with suitable conditions for work, play, recreation, and social life. It is necessary that children learn the great moral lessons involved in work. This points toward the incorporation of a large industrial feature into our conception of school. The need is not merely or primarily that of furnishing vocational training. It should be directed rather toward developing a gradual participation in the real work of the world by the boys and girls while they are in school. These activities should be so invested with the character of real life that the great moral habits will develop from them naturally.

For the activities of play are not merely preparation for life; they constitute actual living at the time, and the process is a real one. This same reality should be carried over into the activities of school. Life in school should be actual life in the stage at which the child finds himself. School experiences should be not only representative, but actual. The various definite things learned by the child should be learned in connection with an activity which is desirable in itself. Spelling is now taught incidentally, in connection with writing. It becomes a means to an activity which actually interests the child. In some schools arithmetic is taught in connection with measurements of trees and other natural objects. In one of the New York schools a year was given to the study of the city water system. The boys were taken to visit the reservoir; they learned the engineering, sanitary, and geographical problems; they clamored for a table of measurements which would enable them to go more fully into the subject.

An inductive study of the spontaneous interests of the child is worth while for education, not merely or chiefly from the standpoint of making school life pleasant for the child, but because the really great intellectual achievements must be done from desire. Education is accomplished largely by the child himself. In the very earliest years the child learns of his own initiative. His parents may spend time teaching him to talk or walk, but the great bulk of his learning is done by the child himself. He learns by suggestion and imitation, based on instinctive tendencies. Think of the labor that would be involved in explaining to every child how to smile. What frightful smiles we should see! Smiling and many similar achievements

PLAY AND EDUCATION 181

are the result of spontaneous activity on the part of the child, directed through selective imitation in accordance with the traditions of his kind.

The place of conscious direction in education is to furnish the time, place, and materials which will draw out the best interests of children. We must build upon the child's instinctive tendencies so that these shall blossom into the best intellectual life, rather than drive the interests by force at a time when we think them appropriate. Now children seem to spend the years from seven to twelve in accomplishing with great difficulty achievements which are done with ease a little later on. We take from the children time that is needed for growth, for the establishment of physical health and bodily skill and the related intellectual activities, and put it upon abstract subjects such as mathematics and grammar, which are forgotten with the greatest ease and rapidity. It is not the place of conscious teaching to make children do at a particular time with infinite pains what they would do with delight at another time. It is not the place of conscious processes to attempt to force the physical or mental education of the child. It is our place to study the orderly development that nature adopts whenever there is opportunity, and to relate our subjects and habits of study to that development so that the child shall be brought most easily into sharing the best life of the past and present.

In order to do this, a careful inductive study of the spontaneous plays of children is necessary. It is perhaps the most fundamental criticism to be passed on Froebel's theory of play that he made no inductive study of this kind. He was keenly sensitive to the educational value of play, and voiced new and epoch-making ideas. But when he actually chose the plays for his kindergarten, he did not study the spontaneous plays that have gone on among children. He thought out a theory of play, and made a curriculum of various plays to produce certain results. In consequence, many of the kindergarten plays do not go of themselves. They are played only so long as the child is under the direction of the teacher. They have not really aroused the child's interest and desire.

It is said that repetition produces habit and character, but we know that this is not true. Desire produces habit. Making a boy brush his teeth every morning for ten years will not make him brush his teeth one more morning if he does not wish to do it. Habits of action

PLAY AND EDUCATION 183

and of thought are the result of the great instinct feelings moulded by tradition until they grow into the living structure of human character. Educators have repeatedly recognized this fact when they have said that the end of education was not to impart information, but to arouse the desire for knowledge. But they have not realized the full implication of this statement. Desire is aroused only along the line of the great instinct feelings, and it is guided by group tradition. These are also the forces dominant in the child's spontaneous play. A careful study of the plays of children will give valuable and authoritative suggestions for the future development of education.

CHAPTER XIV

PLAY AND MORAL GROWTH

THE spontaneous plays of children are significant not alone from the standpoint of their relation to the physical growth of the child, but also from the standpoint of his gradually growing social relations. From this point of view the most noticeable fact about the plays of the baby is their individualistic character. During the first months of life come the spontaneous kickings and all the great body movements, which form the play life of the growing infant. Then he progresses rapidly to playing in more complicated ways. He learns to pick up objects and drop them, to play with sand, blocks, pieces of wood, sticks, anything on which he can use his fingers. He will take delight in running from one place to another, tossing his arms about as he goes. Later he acquires a desire to throw, and the possession of a ball brings delight. Cutting with scissors or a knife is the basis of a whole group of play activities. Swinging and seesaw in various forms begin to interest him.

PLAY AND MORAL GROWTH

All these activities are individualistic, and there is little if anything of the game character about them. If very small children are induced to engage in a game of tag, they show surprisingly little desire to avoid being "it." I have even known them to change quite voluntarily, one assuming the part of being "it" when the other was tired. Games have a definite programme and conclusion, which these plays lack. Moreover, the earlier activities are common not only to children, but to the higher animals as well.

The early play period is devoted to the acquirement of self-mastery in its simplest sense. The child is then learning the fundamental neuro-muscular co-ordinations, and is acquiring a system of reflexes. This is to the baby an intensely interesting process. He may have no desire to do something better than another baby has done, but he enjoys doing something that he himself has done over and over again. If the action of an adult has called forth some new movement from a small child, the insistent cry of "Do it again," is repeated until it becomes a nightmare. The child is forming habits of co-ordination.

This is the time for the acquirement of the reflexes that are not only related to the best life of the child at the period, but those upon which the rightcousness of later life must be built. I refer to such matters as truthfulness, obedience, care of the body, cleanliness. The child must also learn to control his actions; he is acquiring skill and mastery. Loyalty, devotion of the self to the whole, is of small worth if there is no strong, well-managed self to devote.

Interest in the mastery of things and in the increase of power remains throughout life. It may be overshadowed by larger interests, but it is never lost. A man who spends time later in life learning to play the violin finds that a large part of his enjoyment comes from the sense of added dexterity which he gains. He can do something new with his hands; and the sense of additional power is very pleasant. People who learn languages late in life have the same feeling. Even the skill acquired in running a new kind of motor may produce it. I did a little reading in the mathematics of the fourth dimension; at first my mind refused utterly to entertain the idea; it was confusing, unimaginable. But when I began to master the conception, and to see what could be done with it, the added insight was a great source of enjoyment. My sense of the world was enlarged.

Power over one's self, whether it relates to

PLAY AND MORAL GROWTH

strength of muscles, skill, endurance, mental or moral achievement, is a source of joy. To be able to ride a horse or a bicycle, or walk a tight-rope, to swing Indian clubs three-fourths time with one hand and two-fourths with the other —these are small sources of pleasure, but very real ones; and they have a direct connection with moral development. The same growth through new achievements will be found in the baby's play activities. He is acquiring the mastery of his physical mechanism: this is related to all self-control.

After mastery of the self comes the competitive period, which means the mastery of others. This period begins at different ages with different individuals; seven is perhaps nearest the average age. At that time it is no longer sufficient for the boy to throw a stone better than he himself has thrown it before; he wants to throw it farther and straighter than the other boy. This is the beginning of competitive games—not team games, but those involving competition of one individual with another.

The great group of complex tag plays has its place here. The ball games, of which the most common are "One old cat" and "Rounders"; the marble games, varying in details all over the country; racing in its various forms, throwing in competition, jumping and pole-vaulting in competition, and the whole group of track and field sports acquire interest at this age. There are many throwing and running games not included on the chart, because of the lack of space: "Duck on the rock," "Puss in the corner," "Blind man's buff," "Leap-frog," "Mumble the peg." These interests are not lost in after-life, though they are in many respects overshadowed by the great team games. A comparison of the intensity of interest felt in most colleges concerning track athletics and the football team will illustrate this fact.

A friend of mine made a trip to the South. During his stay there he won a tennis championship. When I saw him on his return there were matters of serious import to discuss; he was president of the Public Schools Athletic League and one of the prominent lawyers of the city. But the first fact he mentioned, which evidently gave him great joy, was that he had won a tennis championship when he was twenty-five years older than any of his competitors. This zest in competition continues to old age, under many forms. Even scholarship is not merely the abstract pursuit of learning; it takes account of competition and the superiority of one individual over another.

PLAY AND MORAL GROWTH

This group represents higher interests than those which come at an earlier age; there are more complex intellectual activities involved, more complicated muscular movements, a higher degree of foresight. Many of the movements of this group lead to reflexes of a high order. The effect of tradition begins to make its appearance here, for play has become social in character. The particular games played may vary greatly, far more than do the activities of the first group. The tradition of the group of boys determines the direction that the interest of the individual shall take.

The morality developed during the years of competition is legal, individual, combative. The greatest indignation is felt by the small boy in that period at any one who violates his rights, who will not play by the rules of the game, who fails to observe the law of justice. For him it is "an eye for an eye, a tooth for a tooth." If a boy punches him, it means a punch back. That to him is right, inalienably right. This is the Old Testament period. It is not the time for self-sacrifice, but the time for the establishment of justice. I do not mean that there should be no co-operation or courtesy during this time, because these must begin in babyhood and continue throughout life; but the great achievement that must happen during those years is the setting of the moral backbone. This is fair and that is not fair; this is cheating and that is not cheating. A boy's sense of fair play is at this period his most precious moral asset, and few boys lack this sense. It must be developed and emphasized most strongly at this time. We occasionally meet persons in whom many of the later virtues of self-sacrifice and yielding to the group have never been balanced by this earlier sense of fundamental honor and fairness. They have no beliefs to hold, no conception of what constitutes justice; their attitude toward life is one of continuous concession to everything. To live wholly for others is impossible, because we must eat, sleep, and obtain clothing. A man who does not live for himself, to a certain extent, cannot live for his family or his community. In the same way, a man who has not acquired a firm concept of justice and simple honesty cannot make up for this deficiency by any of the more complex virtues. He lacks the moral fibre that makes a strong, well-balanced character.

There is, however, a more comprehensive morality that comes in with the team games. Here enters the element of devotion to the

PLAY AND MORAL GROWTH

whole, of loyalty to a group. It begins at about the age of twelve, although, in this case also, there are individual variations. As a rule, it is quite futile to plan team games for the years from seven to twelve. Basket-ball played by small children is not team-play. Every one wants to put the ball into the basket himself. The age at which the boy will take another boy's punishment without telling, when he will surrender his own will to the will of the gang, is the age at which a wider morality is beginning, although the symptoms of it are not always lovely. The boy who will go back on his crowd is setting himself against the most profound ethical impulse that these years can develop. This may not be subtle ethics; but it is a fundamental and primary fact.

Team-work is the keynote of this group of games. And team-work is very different from simple co-operation, as any boy who has played on a team knows. A game in which every boy plays as well as he can, but without sacrificing himself for the good of the whole, is not team-work. Rowing, even when done by a group, is not team-work in its most complex sense. One member does not suffer loss in order that his side may win. The sacrifice-hit in baseball is one instance of the kind of play demanded for the good of the team. The members of the group work for the same end, but they do not all do the same thing. Co-ordination and self-sacrifice are the two major elements of this group of games. These games also involve the pursuit of a distant end by means of definite steps, in a more or less definite programme. They involve obedience to a leader, even when he is mistaken. They involve also a higher form of self-mastery than any preceding group, for they demand the despising of pain and individual discomfort for the sake of the cause. These qualities are the beginning of the altruism on which a complex civilization must depend.

A study made of some children who had been brought up apart from others and had never learned to play team games showed some significant facts. They were children of missionaries living with their parents in foreign lands. Their home environment was of the best, but having had no other children with whom they could play, they had played only with their parents. When the period of foreign residence had extended to sixteen years for any child, it was observed that he did not understand the significance of team-play. These children did not learn the tremendous lesson of

PLAY AND MORAL GROWTH

the subordination of the individual to the group. They had learned the lessons of individual righteousness, but had failed to acquire ideas of social righteousness, which do not come through studying a book, but through tradition brought to fruition by action.

One of the great lessons that boys must learn is that there is something larger than the individual self. It is pleasant when playing basket-ball to make a brilliant play for oneself; it is pleasant to be the hero who makes the home run in baseball. But no team that is made up of individuals looking for their own glory ever wins in any of the great collegiate sports—any more than a community can succeed where each citizen works solely for personal interest. This lesson the boy must learn by experience; and he learns it, partly at least, in playing a team game. If a boy plays baseball and does not know the difference between playing for himself and playing for the team, his mates will teach him very promptly and with more energy than any other method could provide.

For play not only expresses the growing moral standards of the boy, it is also a great force in the development of these standards. The social traditions expressed by the play of a group of boys has a far more powerful effect in determining the standards of individual members than has parental authority or reasoning. The team games develop respect for law, in a rudimentary form, to be sure, but in a form capable of growth. The boy that is caught cheating or lying to his own crowd is ostracized. He may lie to others, to his teachers or parents, but he cannot lie to his mates with impunity. The boy learns then that while it is very desirable to win, it is worse to win and forfeit public favor than not to win at all. The essential rules, even of later life, are not written in the statute-books; they are expressed in public opinion.

When the instinct for the gang develops, partisanship may become very violent. This may take various forms. There may be clubs or secret societies. But whatever the form of the combination, the gang is the group of boys who hang together, who sink their individuality in the crowd, who will all fight together if any member is attacked, who do for the group what they would not do for themselves; they feel an allegiance to a cause greater than they themselves. Boys' gangs may very well do better than to fight the policemen, as they do in the city of New York. But whether its oc-

PLAY AND MORAL GROWTH 195

cupations are good or bad with reference to society, from the standpoint of the gang itself loyalty is the fundamental virtue.

This loyalty developed out of play relations and enforced through play traditions may or may not grow into a wider altruism truly moral in that it is truly and completely social. The direction of development will depend largely upon the nature of the group traditions transmitted through play. Here is the opportunity for the teacher who can come into play as a member, rather than as a director. When Judge Lindsey put his arm about a boy and went out to find what the shack was that the boy wanted, and for which he stole the lumber, and why he wanted the sand—he gave something besides sympathy, although that was profound; there was something else than belief in the boy, although that was fundamental. If I understand that boy at all, there arose in him a consciousness that he had come into "playing the game" with the man.

There is great need in the guidance of free play for teachers who know what play is, who understand the force of the instinct feelings involved and the way in which play traditions are formed. Forced play does not change character. Free play, even though there be an adult playing, has the power of modifying character profoundly. And the master of the school who can go out on the grounds and play genuinely with his boys, and be the medium of carrying high athletic traditions, is moulding instinct feeling into the fine form of character.

CHAPTER XV

INSTINCT AND TRADITION IN PLAY

IT is a striking fact that games built on the same fundamental instinct feelings differ among different nations. Even in the case of two peoples as closely related as the English and the American we find this difference. Cricket and soccer football are typical English games, baseball and American football typical American games. Soccer football is the open game in which the ball is kicked, and it is different from our football. Cricket and baseball also differ, not merely in superficial rules, but in the type of play demanded. The ball is in both cases of the same shape. Both games are played on a flat turf. The difference is not physiological. In both games we have the activities of running, catching, and striking. Both depend upon the ability to throw hard and straight, to judge quickly, and to make accurate muscular co-ordinations.

The first noticeable characteristic of a cricket match to an American is the length of time it takes. The movement of cricket is slow; a good match is never played in a day. One person may make a hundred runs. The movement of baseball, on the other hand, is rapid; a game takes at most a few hours. The pitching and catching, the running for bases, the sides coming in and going out—these happenings follow in quick succession. Baseball is the game of an impatient man; it is a driving, restless, pushing game. It allows no pauses. Cricket is a leisurely, gentlemanly, patient, long-continued game. It requires the same kind of skill as baseball, but not the same constant activity. These differences seem to point to basal differences between English and American life.

The origin of baseball is uncertain. Some authorities believe that it grew out of "Rounders," others that it came from "One old cat." But whatever its starting point, baseball has become the great American game, because it expresses American feeling, as cricket is the great English game, because it expresses English feeling. And if we should find that social traditions expressed in play are among the great moulders of character, we must expect that the boy who plays baseball will be shaped, to that extent, toward American life, and the boy who plays cricket toward English life.

It seems evident from this fact that there is

some other factor in play besides the instinctive desire to throw, run, and perform various other acts. If our games were based on instinct feelings alone, unmodified by any other force, there would seem to be no reason for these wide differences in games which call for the same physiological co-ordinations. It would seem, moreover, that the children of every generation would be able to invent all their games afresh from their own developing instincts, that a boy might be able to play baseball without ever seeing the game played, simply because he had the set of instinct feelings that go into the playing of ball.

As a matter of fact, opinions not very much at variance with this view-point have been held. In a warm debate in the House of Representatives with reference to an appropriation for playgrounds in the city of Washington, one congressman said that it was "as necessary and important to teach children to play as to teach the lambs to gambol on the sunny hillsides." He expressed a wide-spread opinion that all play is alike, that children can be trusted to manufacture their own games.

But it is not true even of animals that they play without being taught. There are, it is true, some instincts of life which seem perfect at birth and act without reference to social inheritance or tradition. When a cocoon hatches into a butterfly, it has a set of full-fledged reflexes. It needs no experience; it flies as well at first as later. An instinct of this kind remains unchanged by teaching; it is not plastic. But as we come higher in the animal scale, many instincts lose their fixed character.

Professor Scott of Princeton University experimented extensively with reference to the extent to which the instincts of young birds develop without the aid given by the example of their parents. He raised blackbirds from the eggs, and gave them no opportunity to come in contact with older birds of their kind. They had throats like those of other blackbirds, but they never heard the song of their species. The only noise they heard, which their throats were adapted to copying, was the crowing of a near-by bantam rooster. The result was that the young blackbirds came as near giving a crow like that of the bantam rooster as the nature of their throats permitted. They had an instinct to make a noise, but that instinct developed through imitation. The song of the meadow-lark and the song-sparrow varies so much in different parts of our land that it is possible to identify birds from various sections

INSTINCT AND TRADITION

by the character of their song. It seems probable that this is attributable to the fact that the young copy their song from the old birds, and that variations in different localities perpetuate themselves, passing along from bird to bird.

Scotch terriers have a peculiar way of grasping the hind leg of an opponent in a fight. This has been said to be instinctive; but careful observers have noticed that Scotch terriers not brought up with Scotch terriers do not learn this trick. It is acquired by dogs through playing with the mother, and, in common with the main habits of every dog, is passed along from generation to generation by social inheritance. The otter is one of the most perfect swimmers among land animals, and it would seem as if its instincts must be adapted to water. Yet the young otter dreads the water, and it is necessary, in order that it shall learn to swim, to entice it into the river on the back of its mother, who then plunges under. The animal is thus forced to swim against its will; but, having acquired the habit, it soon learns to enjoy it.

Among savage tribes, children play constantly in the presence of older children and their parents. Initiation ceremonies are common among all primitive peoples. The boys to be initiated into the race ceremonies of their kind are taken apart for a month, or series of months, to learn tribal secrets, the ancestral mode of worship, the sacred language. The boys do not perform these ceremonies by themselves. The rites are in charge of some man who knows them all, and who passes along to the boys this precious inheritance of social tradition that characterizes their people and makes them different from other tribes.

Social tradition is the great shaping force in most of our racial differences. There is in all babies the instinctive tendency to make sounds, but the language that the baby will talk depends on the social inheritance into which he comes. All peoples have an instinctive feeling for shelter, but the houses built are not all of one type. Why do we have standard loaves of bread? The Japanese have other kinds of loaves. Why do men wear one type of hat and women another? Whether it is the form of language we use, the shape of a loaf of bread, the coloring of a hat, the way men may speak to each other and women may speak to each other—all these things are determined not by actual physical heredity, but by the no less firm grasp of social heredity. We may be capable, free individuals, but we are held by laws of tradition which de-

INSTINCT AND TRADITION 203

termine the direction in which our feelings shall express themselves, what we may do and what we may not do.

We are told that the graduates of Yale differ from the graduates of Harvard in certain fundamental respects. If this is true, the difference is not attributable to the fact that the Harvard professors know more Latin than do the Yale professors, or that the Yale professors are better informed on mathematics, philosophy, chemistry, or physics, or any other subject whatever. Neither is it true that such differences in the character of the students coming from these two institutions are traceable to differences in the organization of the institutions. The character of the boy that is being shaped into the character of the man is developed largely by social traditions, passed along from generation to generation of student life. We are told that in the great public schools of England—Rugby, Harrow, and Eton—there are differences in standards and ideals, in the character of the students, in the way they look at life. These are arrived at by the way in which the great school traditions take the raw material of life and shape it constantly and steadily into the form that is characteristic of that institution. Civilized life is something other than mere individual development; it is the force of social tradition that makes civilized life possible.

These same agencies determine the form of children's plays. A boy has a tendency to run and throw, but the particular running and throwing games he will play are determined by the traditions of his people. Games come down without essential change in any stable community, because they are passed from child to child, from the older to the younger. When we speak of the traditions active in play, we are speaking of one of the great controlling forces in all human action. Authority and reason are impotent compared with tradition. The great tragedies of adult life are produced when reason comes in conflict with tradition, when certain actions seem rational and other actions are in accord with social conventions. The same tragedy comes to every boy when the commands of his parents oppose the traditions of the gang. It is the exceptional boy who does not feel the pull of gang custom more strongly than the command of authority. This holds also for us as adults. Whatever we may be told about the unhygienic nature of modern clothing, for instance, we shall hardly be prevailed upon to change our costumes immediately in any striking manner. We prefer to do as the crowd does.

INSTINCT AND TRADITION 205

The way to influence play and the development of the individual that takes place through play is to combine the instinct feelings and the play traditions instead of opposing them.

One of the most interesting examples of the intelligent use and direction of the play instinct feelings is an experiment carried on by Mr. Ernest Thompson Seton. He has an establishment of Indian tribes for boys. All the things that Indians do are done by the boys. They have their mode of government, laws, and a totem-pole. The boys get their names in the manner in which the Indians got theirs, from their looks or from something they have accomplished. They are taught to make tepees. They have games of deer and bear hunts. The bear in these cases is a boy with a balloon on his back. There are three dens about a hundred yards apart to which the bear can retreat. Of course, as there are three caves, the hunter does not know in which one the bear may be hiding. In hunting him the boys have clubs made of light sticks wound with straw, with which they can hit without hurting. If a boy can whack the balloon and break it, he has killed the bear. There is also a system of scouting, of man hunting, and rabbit hunting. There are many honors—small and large—for boys under fourteen years old. They receive feathers for athletic prowess—not for beating some one else, but for attaining some absolute record.

The boys are fascinated with this Indian play. They will submit to a rigid system of discipline, as rigid as that of boys in gangs, and yet not feel that they are under discipline at all. There are many hundreds now of these tribes of "Indians" organized in connection with Mr. Seton's movement. The organization is an adaptation of the outdoor life of Indians to the conditions of the boy, and is the outcome of long years of experiment. Mr. Seton has learned how to make use of the instinctive desires of the boy in reinforcing the traditions and standards which he wishes to impress. He has learned the proper method of play control.

All play is controlled in one way or another. Only the child who is absolutely alone is ungoverned by the rules of the game. When children play tag, no child is free to do as he pleases. The game is controlled by mutual consent. The rigor demanded by this control may exceed any imposed by external authority. The supervision of older children over younger, of mothers over their children, of the whole community over the young, is a well-nigh universal fact. The community is relatively safe

INSTINCT AND TRADITION

from moral disaster as long as the young people play and dance in the presence of their elders; but society is in danger whenever the young go off by themselves unsupervised, for then the control which is inevitable will be in the hands of the inexperienced or even of the vicious.

One of my friends has a boy about nine years old, with whom from his birth the doctrine of "hands off" has been carried out. In consequence he is a nuisance to himself, to his mother, his father, and to all their friends old and young. The boy's instinct feelings have never been curbed, and control has not been acquired. He has never learned what it means to come into conflict with another personality and be answered back in kind. He has learned that he can do anything he pleases with people, and that there are no consequences. To be sure, he knows that if he puts his hand into a flame he will be burned; but he has not been allowed to learn that if he puts his hand against another individual, he will also be burned. The parents of that boy have done him incalculable harm, because they have not allowed him to acquire the great fundamental lessons of human relationships. That boy will go to college, and there he will learn a great deal.

Aside from the influence of older people in

the playing of games, the child learns much through association with his playmates. He is not coming into a world of separate individuals, but into a world of social relationships, and play is the great carrier of social traditions. As soon as one child begins to play with another, that other necessarily limits his freedom. And the limitations are themselves sources for the increase of enjoyment. The instinctive desires to run, throw, strike, begin to be shaped in accordance with the "rules of the game." This shaping means an increase of power, because it brings increased definiteness and correspondence with the social environment. The idea of free play unmodified by playmates, parents, and teachers is a truly pernicious one.

The force of social tradition operating through play has sometimes been deplored. It is said that blind imitation detracts from individuality, and that children are deprived of all initiative by stimulating their desire to follow an example. But unconscious imitation is not a blind force; it is very selective. When a new football player comes to town, nine out of ten of the boys of the town will at once copy him as nearly as they can in attitude of body, expression of face, tilt of hat or cap. But when a boy walks down the street and sees a willow-tree waving

INSTINCT AND TRADITION

its branches, he does not stand and balance and commence imitating the willow-tree. There is something in the football player that makes the boy want to imitate, something that responds to his ideal, that arouses a desire in him to be like his kind. There is nothing in the tree to call forth a similar stimulus. Expose a thousand boys to the power of music, and only those who have special capacity for music will respond. This imitation, conscious of kind, enormously selective, apparently making for likeness, is really an agency which brings out individual differences.

One other objection is frequently made to the conscious use of play as a carrier of tradition. We are told that it is "unnatural" to interfere with children, that they must be left to develop freely according to their "nature." But the instinctive desire to teach is as natural as any other desire. The father wants to teach his boy to throw, to shoot with the bow, to hunt, to paddle, to swim. The mother instinctively desires to take the baby in her arms and to sing to it. These feelings are as natural as any other feelings. If human instincts are to be allowed to develop freely, then the mother and father instincts must also be considered.

There is apt to be great confusion as to what

is natural. We hear of a natural food cult which claims that since man's body grew up under conditions of nature, the special preparation of food by cooking, which man himself has developed, is artificial, and therefore undesirable. In this narrow sense of the word natural, the best possessions of human kind are unnatural. The wearing of garments is artificial; the building of houses is wholly unnatural; it would be natural to crawl into caves. The ventilation of houses is unnatural; heating is exceedingly unnatural. Education is, of course, above all unnatural—as morals are unnatural.

But in the wider sense of the word, we must consider natural those things which have survived and approved themselves in the course of evolution. We have reached that stage of development where human affairs are being increasingly directed by conscious effort. That state of control is natural now for the human race. We can no longer rely wholly upon the blind forces of instinct, but must deliberately shape those instincts so that they shall operate in accord with general human needs and be of service to mankind.

CHAPTER XVI

PLAY AND OUR CHANGING CIVILIZATION

SOME years ago the University of Missouri introduced a bill in the State Legislature asking for $100,000 for the building and equipment of a gymnasium. The hardheaded, conservative legislators laughed at the proposal. "Why cannot those boys saw wood for exercise, as we did?" they asked. The representatives of the State university waited until the meeting of the next legislature and introduced another bill asking for $200,000 for the erection and equipment of a plant for sawing wood. It was shown that the wood had to be brought from so great a distance, and the loss occasioned by hand-sawing instead of machinery would be so large, that at least as great an endowment as asked for was necessary. The legislators had forgotten the fact that the conditions in which they were brought up have passed away, and that it is no longer possible to educate a boy by muscular work, as muscles do not do the great work of the world to-day. They voted the $100,000 asked for the gymnasium.

The foregoing illustrates only one aspect of the change that has come over modern life. The increasing urbanization of our population is another factor in the problems of our day. We are fast becoming a city people. We have tried the experiment of exporting the dwellers in the crowded tenements. But while we are driving them out of one slum, they return to another. Statistics tell most convincingly the growth of cities. In 1790 3.3 per cent of the people in the United States lived in cities of 8,000 population and upward. To-day, more than 33 per cent live in cities of the same class. This means not only that the cities are growing with phenomenal rapidity, but that the total population growth of our country during the past three censuses has been almost entirely an urban growth. I was told that within a single generation the average country school in Illinois had shrunk from seventy-eight to thirty-eight pupils.

A still larger proportion of our population is bound to become urbanized. It is the necessary consequence of our industrial civilization, where the processes of working up material require vastly more individuals than those of

PLAY AND OUR CIVILIZATION 213

raw production. There is nothing to gain and everything to lose through an attitude of hostility to this tendency. So long as we try to stand out against it, planting ourselves on an old civilization, championing to the last ditch those conditions that are being surely undermined and swept away, we are fighting against the stars in their courses. To talk of "three acres and liberty" for our children is futile. We must accept the city for what it is, necessary, artificial, congested, nervously organized; and we must discover how to make these very traits count in upward development. Not by opposing inevitable tendencies, but by discovering their possibilities for good and pushing these to their logical issues shall we aid in the solution of our greatest social problem.

For this problem is not merely one of the city. This increasing urbanization is but one symptom of the change going on everywhere, a change in the direction of greater organization and specialization. It is not a question of city or country, as we are tempted to think when we compare the farm of a past age with the city of the present. The farm has become as man-made as the city; it is in many respects as specialized in activity. Whole farms are given over to the raising of violets, whole sections of the country to the raising of wheat. The change is one in the texture of modern life. It makes no difference whether a boy's father runs a trolley-car, is president of a bank, owns a wheat-farm, sells goods behind a counter—the work of the modern man, except in rare cases, is such that it is impossible for the boy to serve an apprenticeship to life's tasks by working with his father. Yet in that way the boys of an earlier generation gained their physical power, health, and moral responsibility.

The farms in the old days were of the all-around character. The children were obliged to help their parents spin the thread. They wove, dyed, cut out the cloth. They made the garments; they even made the patterns. They made their hats, and sometimes even their shoes. They made their farming utensils, both of wood and iron. The boy thus secured a training such as is given in no manual training school to-day. I am not now speaking of the pleasurable side of childhood, for I am well aware that a boy's hands will blister much more quickly on a hoe handle than on a baseball bat. But a hoe handle is an instrument of exercise of a genuine sort, and it does result in power of the arms and back, in ability to digest food. We have taken from our boys not merely the work, but the physical and moral results that come from it.

During a brief period it was my privilege and obligation to work on a farm. I arose at four o'clock in the morning to get the cows, of which I milked seven twice a day. That was exercise for the hands. I had to care for the milk and wash the cans. Then came the regular farm work. I was not old enough to plough, but I had to handle a horse rake, and there were many chores. I helped to fill the woodshed, to build stone and wooden fences, and to dig out woodchucks. I helped thresh the wheat and brought it in, husked the corn, and did the other jobs that are to be done on an all-around farm. My boy cannot do these things at home; there is no opportunity for him.

In still other ways has the relation of the child to the community been modified. The family has hitherto always been the chief unit of society. But during the past century the relation of the family to society has changed profoundly in all civilized communities. Many functions of the old family unit are now being performed by the community in other and mainly better ways. The features of this change most vital to our subject are disclosed in the statement that until recently the home has been the place (*a*) where children learned to work with their parents, (*b*) where they secured most of their education, (*c*) where they obtained their religious and moral training, (*d*) where they centred most of their social life.

A great deal of work has gone out of the home. Everywhere the family is ceasing to be the centre of the industries of the world. Walking behind one of the great steam gang-ploughs drawing sixteen ploughs, each cutting three inches deep and sixteen inches wide, one can see that there is no place here for the boy to take the lines of the horses and to co-operate with his father. Articles are now made in the shop or the factory, and not in the home. The boy can no longer help his father in the practice of trades. He has no chance to make things, no tools to make things with, no materials out of which to make them, and no place to keep any things he might make. The modern home affords no opportunity for the growing boy to exercise his constructive impulses in a wholesome way.

The situation is just as difficult for the girl. It has been one of the problems in our family to discover necessary, useful work for our girls; it is hard to find work that cannot be done better by some one else; and it is not only hard, but unjust, to require girls to do work merely

PLAY AND OUR CIVILIZATION 217

for the sake of doing it. We are willing to give help where help is needed, but to work for the sake of its subjective effect alone gives no permanent solution of the problem. And a large part of the necessary work, even of women, is leaving the home. Few people to-day bake their own bread; many no longer bake even their own cake. Underwear is no longer made in the house. Outside clothing is usually made away from the home.

Education is leaving the home. Practically all the formal instruction that children now receive is given in school. In the old days there were schools, to be sure, but they did not begin so early, nor did they last so many months out of the year, nor so many years out of the children's lives. The school which takes all the children of the country from the ages of six to fourteen and compels them under penalty to be incarcerated in the schoolroom from nine o'clock in the morning until three o'clock in the afternoon, five days a week for nine or ten months in the year, is a new institution and has materially altered the lives of children. No change equal in magnitude has ever occurred in the lives of the young of any other living species.

The home is no longer the centre of religious and moral instruction. An investigation made in New England some years ago with reference to family worship and the asking of the blessing at meals revealed the fact that these practices had been all but abandoned even among church members and regular attendants at church. This was true in the city of Springfield, Massachusetts, a community not yet disturbed in its traditions by the mixing of many kinds of people. Yet its homes had been practically stripped of the old-time religious practices. In the past the home has been the centre of religious instruction, ever since the time when the father was the high priest of the family and the mother tended the fire that was never allowed to go out. Now we have organized young people's societies, young men's and young women's Christian associations, and many other institutions of religion. These are accomplishing what the home never accomplished. They are influencing the actions of the masses in a way in which the home never influenced them.

Yet the difficulty is, if a boy does not learn moral conduct from the example and traditions in his home, it cannot be given to him by any precept or discourse. The power of social tradition is not to be overcome or supplanted by reasoning, but only by other social tradition. The principal of a large eastern school said to

PLAY AND OUR CIVILIZATION 219

me: "What would you do if a boy came to you who had been lying, one of the brightest boys in the school? When I talked to him and told him how the whole community despised a liar, he said: 'I don't believe a word you say. My father is a liar, my mother is a liar, and my sister is a liar. My father is a thoroughly successful business man of high standing and great wealth, and I do not believe that the whole community despises a liar. It is only fools that tell the truth all the time.' And his father *was* a brilliant man, and his mother *was* a woman of culture and she *was* a liar; all those things were true that the boy was telling."

Habits of conduct cannot be inculcated by right instruction. Right living is not transmitted by telling children to be honest and true and brave. It is developed in the individual as a phase of other activities, and through the example of parents and other adults working, playing, and carrying on their social life together with the children. The transmission of morals is no longer safe in the family because the activities out of which morals arise have been taken away. I do not mean that the family has degenerated or deteriorated. But the community has taken over many of the functions that the family formerly had. The moral problems facing the father and mother are not the kind into which the children can enter as they did in the past. In the case of the clerk, the bank president, the trolley-car conductor, the moral questions are technical and of a kind that do not lend themselves to general family example. When children worked with their parents they had opportunity to adjust themselves gradually to the world's work and the obligations of adult life.

To remedy the situation we must look forward and not backward. It is as impossible as it would be undesirable to restore the old family industries. There are a number of societies in America that are trying to reintroduce handicraft in the family, and thus to solve this and certain other problems. That is to restore by looking backward. To call the father from the railroad or the shop, from the specialized farm, the store or the bank, and have him again live the long wasteful hours of unspecialized labor, to have the mother again become the slave of toil in order to create the rude home necessities of a century ago, all this is foolish and impossible. We have passed that stage.

Play is leaving the home. The family life has always been the centre of children's play. In the case of small children it is so still. But the home is no longer the centre of activities, and children want to be where something is going on; so as they grow older, they go out on the street where things are happening, and have their play and social life there. The school has become for many the centre of companionship. The city home is too small for any great number of children to come in and play. Children less and less have their parties at home, not merely because the home is not large enough—the home is no longer the centre of the activities that make up social life.

We are not to face this conclusion with pain and regret; that is the attitude of most of us when we think of the home. We speak in despairing voices and in a dejected manner, and there is no hope in us. But the condition that we face is not one of irreparable loss. It is not even a second best that I am proposing. I believe in the home, but I believe more in the individual and the community. We are to conserve only the features of the home that are best for us, and we must let others go, one after the other, to the community, as soon as it is clear that it is best for all to do so.

We have gained greatly by performing in the community many of the things formerly done in the home. This is notably true in respect to industries and education. Even play, under the best modern conditions, may be better provided by the community than it ever was by the family. Modern play is carried on under the leadership of splendid young men and women who are familiar with the play traditions that have been passed on from generation to generation. By selecting from among us those who are best adapted to be play teachers we may secure for our children a play life which is as much richer than the product of the old average home, as modern education excels the old home education.

Industry has been organized in a wonderful way, and the material progress of the day is related to this fact. Education too has been highly organized. We have not merely the general school-teacher, but specialists of all kinds, who are giving much better instruction than the mother ever gave. But recreation remains the one great activity in America which has not fully felt that genius for organization which brings to play the advantages of human co-operation so characteristic of this century. We have lost the relation of recreation to the home, but have not fully established its relation to the community. That is the present state of affairs.

We need, then, first of all, an intelligent facing of the problem. We must study our resources. We must deliberately set about knowing what we have to work with—streets, parks, school buildings, roofs. We must know what instincts and social traditions we can count upon. We must formulate some comprehensive plan. A measure such as this is necessary if we are to make sure of equal attention to the needs of every class and avoid that overlapping of energy which always accompanies individual, unconnected efforts. Our cities are being architecturally beautified in accordance with far-seeing, harmonious municipal designs. Our industries are being developed through thorough and effective study of resources and aims. Our physical, moral, and social health should receive the same broad, expert, and centralized treatment.

CHAPTER XVII
PLAY AND THE MODERN CITY

THE ideal home playground is the back yard. What are our ideals concerning it with reference to children? The utility of the yard for play is not directly related to the extent of its area. One eight feet wide and twelve feet long—that is, a very small yard—if it is properly equipped may afford an exceedingly large amount of play for children.

A back-yard swing is always interesting to children. It need not be fifteen feet high in order to give enjoyment, and any one can put up a little swing of three feet. I am not informed as to the kind of feelings that children have in swinging at different heights; but I know that when swinging in a swing twenty or thirty feet high, I have a different state of mind from that which I experience when swinging in a low, short swing about five or six feet in height. My own belief is that, so far as appealing to the interest of children is concerned, the short swing is far more effective than the long one. And yet the fathers and mothers

PLAY AND THE MODERN CITY 225

who wish to do exceptionally well for their children erect large swings which require a definite amount of time to complete the change of direction, whereas what the children want is a quick change of direction.

Then there is the sand pile. It need not be large. An ordinary soap box filled with sand will keep small children happily employed hour after hour. There is no problem of either space or expense which would warrant denying children the joys of a little swing and a sand pile.

Ordinary kitchen ladders were arranged by Mr. Joseph Lee around the sides of a back yard in a way so as to permit children to play tag while swinging from one rung to another of the ladders. In this way they went round and round the yard in their play. This simple apparatus converted the yard into a three-dimension playground. The ladders were arranged in a manner so that the children could mount and dismount them easily, and would run small danger from possible falls.

The possibilities of block and structural plays in the back yard have already been described. The only trouble with our own little back yard in Brooklyn, where we kept a supply of these building-blocks, was that the yard was always swamped with children. During all the hours of daylight children were found there. Even when we were away the children of the neighborhood would climb over the fence and play there all day.

Thousands of poor little rich children parade on Riverside Drive in New York every day, holding their nurses' hands, or merely walking or running about within range of the nurse's voice. These children do not want an airing; they want to play, but there are no back yards for the poor little rich children. Is it not possible to multiply these back-yard playgrounds in our city life?

I question whether what we are doing for children in providing play opportunity in our cities is, in the nature of the case, adequate. We now use the surface of the ground twenty times over for purposes of business, but for a playground we use it only once. The mode of making manifold use of the ground for business has been evolved as the result of much labor and intensive study. Corresponding study and effort have not yet been given to creating conditions which will provide as adequately for child life in our cities. To give children in the congested parts of old and large cities adequate playgrounds involves so great a degree of reconstruction as to render such an attempt prac-

PLAY AND THE MODERN CITY

tically impossible. The solution of this problem lies in the future. One suggestion that has occupied and fascinated me is a many-storied playhouse, of twenty stories, perhaps. But a playhouse, strictly speaking, placed in a solid block of other buildings, would not be adequate to the needs of child life because of the lack of sunshine and air. The plan may be feasible, however, if the house is constructed with open sides, after the manner of our recreation piers. The twenty-story play-pier is a structure of the future.

The church may help in meeting the play situation. When it throws open the gates of its beautiful grounds in order that within the enclosure the people and children of the neighborhood may have opportunities to play, this action will stand as a symbol of the relationship of religion to life. The spiritual life cannot be lived apart from the world; it includes and envelops the simplest daily work, play, and relationships of life.

If there are times of the day when our parks are not adequately used, it might be brought about that groups of children would then be permitted to play in them. By this I do not mean that the parks should be overrun with children, so as to destroy their beauty, but simply that we need to take an accurate account of all the available facilities at our command in the city, so that the greatest use possible will be made of the undeveloped play possibilities which we possess.

Blocks of city streets may be set aside for the play of children. I have no explanation to offer for the feelings of joy that children obtain from swift running and sliding. Three of my daughters had roller-skates, and the time they spent going up an asphalted street and down again like the wind, with the elation of spirits that resulted, the ecstasy produced in them, seemed to me matters of much wonder. The expression of this exuberance of spirit it is possible to obtain only by the use of a relatively extensive area such as a city block affords.

The community must provide for children to the same extent, and more completely, more intelligently, more fully than the family formerly provided for children—because the community is to have the children. It has them now—and leaves them unprotected on the streets after school hours. That situation must be remedied. Our streets must be made places that are as wholesome for children as are our homes. The very word "home" is tied up with the thought of children, and the time will surely come when the word "city," the larger home, will similarly be tied up with the idea of the care of children. The most important thing in the world is how children grow up. It matters not how splendid is our architecture, how complete are our parks and statues, how fine is our poetry, how perfect our political system —if the children of our families grow up sickly or immoral or poor. The supreme question for every generation to ask itself is: Have you done that which has passed on to the next generation the treasures of life fully, completely, and wholesomely? If you have not, then civilization means nothing, art means nothing, education means nothing, religion means nothing. Religion means nothing unless it means progress toward God, and that means wholesomeness in all aspects of life.

CHAPTER XVIII

DIRECTION AND CONTROL IN PLAY—PLAYGROUNDS

IN 1897 the Park Board of Toledo secured two pieces of ground and installed a complete equipment of playground apparatus. No supervision was provided, the grounds being in charge of the regular park attendants. As a result the apparatus was soon destroyed by rough usage, and the smaller children received such treatment at the hands of older bullies that they did not dare to go near the playgrounds. The grounds were eventually closed on the petition of the people living in the neighborhood, because their influence proved wholly bad. This unfortunate experience caused widespread opposition to later efforts made in Toledo for the establishment of playgrounds. At last a well-regulated playground was established, financed by the Federation of Women's Clubs, and supervised by a leader from the Young Men's Christian Association. The good results obtained from this playground effectually destroyed the opposition.

DIRECTION AND CONTROL 231

The experience of Toledo is not unique. In Duluth, Minnesota, in the spring of 1908, Mayor Haven inaugurated a campaign for playgrounds. An association was formed to secure funds for rental, equipment, and supervision. The local physical director of the Young Men's Christian Association was appointed supervisor. At about this time the Park Board installed a few swings and seesaws in Portland Square, but failed to put the ground under supervision. It immediately became a meeting-place for undesirable boys, especially at night. So much protest came from residents in the vicinity that the apparatus had to be removed. Since then the Park Board has coöperated with the Playground Association in supplying apparatus only to grounds under supervision.

Pawtucket, Rhode Island, had a similar experience. In the spring of 1908 the city authorities decided to experiment with a small playground on a piece of city property centrally located. An appropriation was made for a small amount of apparatus, but supervision was not provided. The place became an exceedingly noisy one and a loafing ground for the rough element of the town. The larger boys monopolized the apparatus. The neighbors protested. The Associated Charities offered to provide a supervisor. This offer was accepted and the work was carried on under that organization for the remainder of the season to the entire satisfaction of the neighborhood.

These examples illustrate one extreme in the attitude toward playground control. The other extreme was shown in Paris, at the time when the value of play first began to be recognized. A good playground was established in connection with a certain school, and the teachers worked out a play curriculum, which should contain all the desired elements. At a given hour the children were marched to the playground in military fashion, and told: "These are your playthings, and such are the games you must play." If they did not obey, they were punished.

This is the type of directed play to which objection is rightly made. But the objection to directed play is frequently carried further. When the Playground Association of America was organized in Washington, President Roosevelt said: "It is a splendid thing to provide in congested districts of American cities spaces where children may play; but let them play freely. Do not interfere with their play. Leave them alone." Later he changed his opinion, but in those words he voiced a general public feeling regarding the whole matter of play and playgrounds, the feeling that children should be let alone, that they will play wholesomely if adults do not interfere. This view can no longer be held in face of the experience of Toledo and other cities. Real freedom is impossible without protection. An unsupervised playground is nominally free; in reality it is controlled by the strongest and most vicious element in the crowd. It is a dangerous place for girls and small children; it can be converted from a direct source of evil to a source of benefit by having some one put in authority, who will see that the ground is used for the purpose for which it was intended—that the older boys have their place and the smaller children theirs, and that each group is free within its own limits. No large company of people can be free without control of this kind.

In addition to this negative protection, free play needs to go one step further in our modern city, or in any place where play traditions are relatively new. If untaught boys are put on parallel bars, they may not know what to do. If they are taken to a swimming-tank and have never learned to swim, they are unable to enjoy themselves. But if a man goes with them who is a good swimmer and diver, who is proficient in the various accomplishments that the boys want to learn, then the example which he sets not only does not interfere with the freedom of their play but makes real play for the first time possible. He is a play promoter. His task is the same as that of the modern librarian, who directs by showing possibilities.

The conditions of modern life have emphasized the necessity of some play example. A young woman came out of a New York settlement one afternoon, and found nearly 200 children crowding around the door. The playground across the street had closed. She asked what they were waiting for. "The Children's Service," was the reply. "What is that?" she asked. "Oh, that's where you sit around and sing. It comes at half-past six." It was only a little after five at the time, and the children were waiting there, standing on the street for more than an hour, until they should have an opportunity to "sit around and sing." They did not have to come early to get a seat. But they had no idea of any way to amuse themselves. They did not know anything to play in the meantime.

In a community that is relatively stable, where one generation of children succeeds an-

DIRECTION AND CONTROL

other almost imperceptibly, each graduating generation can be counted upon to leave play traditions behind it: such and such shall be the games of this community, and played according to this standard; and the legacy is accepted unquestionably. Games handed down in this way have proved well suited to their environment. Thus a game like "Monkey chase," which requires trees and a grassy running space, was an ideal game for an old Connecticut orchard, where it was developed with a most elaborate code of regulations; but it could not bear transplanting to the city. The play tradition was broken, and "Monkey chase" died. The majority of country games has shared the same fate. There is no space to play these games in a large city.

Most of the traditional games of the world have grown up under conditions of plenty of space and plenty of time. Relatively few games can be found that are useful where 500 children are turned out for a ten-minute recess into a yard where 50 can play comfortably. Then some one must come in to modify the old games, so that 50 can play in a given space where only 10 could play before; so that games which once demanded an hour can be played in ten minutes. The old conditions under which the games arose have gone. The games will go also, unless they are adapted to the new conditions. For this also we need the play promoter, the play teacher.

One of the most keenly sought enjoyments of those who visit the older countries is to witness the celebration of national holidays. The national and folk-dances which have grown up around these occasions are the most common form of art available to all the people. Here in America we have the same human feelings demanding expression, we have occasions demanding adequate celebration, but we have no form of social habits. We do not yet know how to celebrate the Fourth of July adequately. We have no appropriate celebration for Lincoln's birthday, or for Thanksgiving Day. We need traditions. Our poverty in this direction is shown when our people come together after some great occasion, such as a state or national election. We have fireworks in some cities; but most people do nothing but surge up and down the streets in hopeless confusion. We have no social forms in which to express our common emotion.

It would seem that in a country like ours, made up of people from many parts of the world, we could be peculiarly rich in all our social inheritances. It would seem as if we would have gathered together all that rich folk-lore which comes down from mouth to mouth, from mother to child, from generation to generation, sometimes carried by the professional story-teller, sometimes by the children themselves, embodying within itself the forms of moral discipline and social relation, and stores of folk music in which the dawning æsthetic sense is shown. We have many people from Norway and Sweden, Russia, Italy, Spain, and Greece. But we have not the folk music, the folk-lore, the folk poetry, the great games which have been elaborated during the experience of the centuries, and which perfectly fitted the children of the communities from which our immigrants came. The children of New York, one of the most cosmopolitan cities in the world, are poverty-stricken in the knowledge of play.

These facts seem to point inevitably to one conclusion. The great traditions of social life are not carried by the individual, or even by the family; they are carried by the community as a whole. It would seem as if the great communities, composed of groups of people from all parts of the world, would inherit the traditions of all; but such is not the case. They inherit only the simplest traditions, the elements common to all. The children of these complex communities play only a few games, the games they all have in common. They will play tag because tag is played everywhere, but not the complex forms of tag. They will dance none of the great dances which have been the first stimulus toward the sense of beauty and rhythm the world over. They may invent some games which suit the conditions in which they find themselves, but they will invent poor games at first.

Craps, a gambling game played with dice, is a typical city game, invented by the children of the city. It is the product of city environment, and it is in many respects admirably adapted to that environment. It is an interesting game; of that there can be no doubt. All the severe steps taken to eliminate it have been in vain. Craps is suited to city conditions. It can be played in a limited space. It is a quiet game; boys playing craps break no windows and do not annoy the neighborhood. It is a game suited to limited time; it can be played in five minutes or five hours. It adapts itself to any number of players, five, ten, or an indefinite number. Craps is the almost inevitable outgrowth of modern city conditions; it bids fair to become the national game of the

DIRECTION AND CONTROL 239

tenements. There are, however, two respects in which craps is not a good game. It is useless physiologically and it is bad morally. It keeps boys crouched in an unwholesome position, and it teaches them to gamble. This is the type of game that our city environment creates and fosters, unless "by taking thought" we provide some better game equally well adapted to the conditions of space and time and opportunity.

The conscious teaching and promotion of play need not take the form of interference. A friend spent his summers in a small country community from which most of the active and energetic young men had gone to the cities. Those left remained for some special reason, or because they lacked initiative. In that particular community no games were being played by the older boys. There was no baseball. The young man referred to was a catcher on the Yale University baseball team. He became acquainted with some of the country boys, who on one Fourth of July asked him if he knew how to play ball. He answered "Yes." So he came out with them, and it was soon evident that he was a good player. They enjoyed playing with him, he organized them, and they elected him captain. When they discovered that he had played in college, he became the great man of the community. After a while he proposed that they should keep up their organization for doing other things besides playing ball. That young man went to them for several years and reshaped the lives of those country boys. He became to them an ideal, and was, no doubt, idealized. He led them in directions that make for power, persistence, clean, strong play. He gave them something to do—and a model.

This is the ideal type of play direction—the control which comes through example and playing together. Through play leaders such as these a transfer is made from generation to generation, not merely of games, but of character. Teachers who play with their children accomplish this type of control to some extent, and the measure of their success lies in the measure in which they themselves play rather than imitate playing. It may be tested by its results. If the children repeat of their own free will the games they have learned on the playground, if they have accepted those plays not under compulsion, but because the games appealed to them, then the play leader has fulfilled his function. The right kind of playground leadership attracts children; a properly supervised playground is always more crowded than an unsupervised play space. To adapt old play traditions and to create new ones suited to the requirements of city life is to set in motion a force the influence of which can hardly be measured.

Doctor Haddon relates an experience in Borneo during a rain-storm when he took refuge in the hut of a native. He found a group of persons waiting, like himself, for the storm to cease. Thinking to amuse the native children, he took a piece of string from his pocket, tied it in the form of a loop, put it on his hands and made a "Cat's cradle." He then showed them how to "take it off." He was surprised that it was taken off promptly. Then he took it off, and this pastime was continued until he came to the end of his series, after which the native children went on for four or five figures more. It is a long time, Doctor Haddon says, since their forefathers and ours dwelt together and as children played "Cat's cradle" together; but upon no other hypothesis is it possible to account for the development and preservation of this form of play, which is too complicated to have been developed twice in just that manner. The children played it and taught it to the younger children; they learned it and taught it to the younger children, they in turn to the younger children, and so on for hundreds and thousands and maybe tens of thousands of years, in an unbroken chain from the time when their fathers and ours lived together.

Such is the force that carries the forms of play, and we in America have seriously interfered with it. That is why the great folk-dances and folk festivals have gone, and why we must teach our children to play. That is why we must make a conscious effort to restore their birthright. Therefore we need tradition carriers, play leaders. Without them it would be better to have no playgrounds at all; that has been the experience in congested districts. With the right kind of play promoter, play is free from the interference of bullies; it is enriched and made more interesting; it then becomes capable of transmitting the social and moral traditions of the race.

CHAPTER XIX

PLAY AND DEMOCRACY

WHEN the baby was learning to creep, she one day discovered the bottom step of the stairs leading to the upper story. The step interested her. Placing her hands upon it, she raised one foot. When this was safely put on the higher level, she endeavored to raise the other foot. While she was doing this, she was followed by her anxious mother and doting father. The latter had brought a sofa pillow and had it ready, so that when the loss of balance came and the toddler rolled backward down the step, she was shocked and frightened, but in no way injured. She had learned the first lesson about climbing and falling.

This policy of allowing children to learn by experience, but safeguarding the experience so that it shall not be disastrous, was pursued with the other children of that family. They spent their summers on the edge of a bluff about forty feet high, with the bank sloping down at an angle of forty degrees. During the summer vacations, although the children had complete freedom—swinging over the bluff on tree branches, going where they pleased down the slope—not one of them, little or big, ever fell, because they had learned the lesson of falling when they were small, and in ways that did not bring disaster.

In a well-managed playground the children are treated in a similar way with reference to their experiences with one another. In addition to receiving the physical benefits that come from wholesome outdoor exercise, and the intellectual benefits that come from useful constructive work, the little children playing on the sand pile learn fundamental lessons in mutual rights. The older children learn lessons in mutual relationships by sharing the use of swings, by having to play by the rules of the game. Later on, as they form into teams, they learn that self-sacrifice which is involved in the team game. They learn that the social unit is larger than the individual unit, that individual victory is not as sweet as the victory of the team, and that the most perfect self-realization is won by the most perfect sinking of one's self in the welfare of the larger unit— the team. Thus the child learns to control

PLAY AND DEMOCRACY

himself in these increasingly complex relationships, and he learns to control himself because he is not externally controlled.

It is true that there is in the playground a measurable degree of control—that kind of control which wards off disaster—as in the case of the baby learning to climb. There is that control which prevents the older from encroaching on the rights of the younger, which restrains the bully from encroaching on the rights of the weaker. But the control in a well-managed playground is largely of the mutual consent kind. It is that control which obtains throughout well regulated society—the control of public opinion, rather than the control of either force or fear.

Play in itself is neither good nor bad. To sink one's very soul in loyalty to the gang is in itself neither good nor bad. The gang may be a peril to the city, as indeed is the case in many cities. The gang of boys that grows up to be the political unit, bent merely upon serving itself, possessing a power which mutual loyalty alone can give, is thereby enabled to exploit others for its own advantage in a way that is most vicious. My point is that these mutual relationships have an ethical effect. This effect may be toward evil and it may be toward good;

but the ethical nature in itself is primarily related to self-control and to freedom.

In some institutions of learning the traditions of athletics are such as to tolerate, and even to approve of conduct and of ways of playing which in other institutions are utterly condemned. The boy going through one institution will come out having ideals with reference to athletics and other things which have been shaped toward good—or toward evil in the other case. Hence the significance of having playgrounds and play organizations, including school athletic organizations, in which the ideals presented shall make for good social relationships that frown on the bully, that exclude the person who is selfish, that approve of the person who is courteous as well as strong and quick—organizations where honesty is recognized and fair play is generally accorded. Anti-ethical play is worse than no play at all. It is not merely play that our cities and our children need; they need the kind of play that makes for wholesome moral and ethical life, the play that makes for those relationships between individuals that will be true to the adult ideals which belong, and should belong, to the community.

There is real freedom on the playground, because the child must either play by the rules

PLAY AND DEMOCRACY

or be shut out by his playmates or those in charge. In this respect the playground is unique. The child is not free to leave school as he pleases. He cannot leave his home as he pleases. Of course, within the limitations of the school and the home there are varying degrees of freedom, but essentially and at bottom there is and must be authority. I am not decrying authority; it is necessary. But I am saying that in addition to authority there must be an opportunity in the life of the child for the development of those qualities which depend upon, and which are developed only under conditions of freedom. This kind of control which people exert upon one another is, to be sure, external control—and external control, we have said, does not develop morality; but this external control of the playground differs from the control of the home or the school in this respect: the child is free to leave it if he chooses. If a boy does not want to play ball in the way that satisfies his comrades, he can get out; he is free. Hence, if he stays, controlling his temper and playing according to the fair ideal of his playmates, there is a kind of self-control that is not exercised either in the school or in the home, where authority is fundamental.

The school and the home must teach obedience as a primary virtue. Obedience is increasingly necessary wherever large masses of persons come together. This is perhaps nowhere better shown than at a fire in a school building. There have been several fires in New York city schools, but in not one has there been loss of life. In not one has a class been stampeded; not a single teacher has fainted or screamed or left her post. In these fires (which might otherwise have resulted in great loss of life) the children have stood quietly in their places—although in some instances the rooms were filled with smoke—until the order came for them to go, when they moved rapidly, quietly, in step, down the precise way which they were told to go. Nothing but plain, straight obedience can meet situations such as these—obedience to authority, immediate, prompt, and all-inclusive.

The child must progress through the grades step by step. It is not his to say when he will study geography and when history or mathematics. These decisions cannot be left to him. It is not his to determine what shall be the school hours, the school vacations. These questions must be settled by persons of far larger viewpoint than he possesses. In a measure the school may be organized so that a certain degree of

PLAY AND DEMOCRACY

co-operation is secured from the pupils, as in the school city; but the fundamental questions of school administration are not for the pupil to decide, and we need not blind ourselves to the fact that the school must be fundamentally and essentially a monarchy; and that it does, should, and must develop primarily the qualities of obedience.

In view of the changing conditions that now obtain, it is a little difficult to discuss the question of obedience in relation to the home. But even under the present conditions it is perhaps safe to say that except in so far as there is obedience to some authority in the home, there is no true home.

Thus the two great institutions that have to deal with children—the school and the home—rest primarily upon the development of the qualities of obedience. The playground alone affords to children the one great opportunity for cultivating those qualities that grow out of meeting others of like kind under conditions of freedom; it develops progressively, from babyhood on, that sense of human relationships which is basal to wholesome living. Thus the playground is our great ethical laboratory.

Where there is no freedom, there can be no self-control. The man whose limbs are shackled cannot control them. The man whose mind is shackled, cannot control his mind. The person who is compelled by force or fear, so that he is not free, has no self-control. The control of one's self is absolutely based upon having the freedom to control one's self—a freedom to do wrong, as well as right. If a boy is made to do a thing by force, he has to do it; he may or may not want to. It is a non-moral proceeding. It may be necessary, but it is not on a moral level. For instance, a boy may have to take quinine. He may object to it so vigorously that his nose must be held in order to open his mouth. This may be good for him, but it has no effect on his morals. He is not free, and freedom is necessary for morality. Self-control of the higher type is primarily developed under the conditions of the playground, rather than under the conditions of the school and the home.

I spoke of that experience which the baby had in learning her early steps—the process of avoiding tumbles. She learned by doing. This is one of the fundamental words of the new education, and it has now come to be applied practically to all the subjects of the school curriculum. The child learns to read by reading. He learns to write by writing. He learns

PLAY AND DEMOCRACY 251

arithmetic by adding, subtracting, multiplying, and dividing. He learns his physics by making experiments. He learns his chemistry in the laboratory. He learns his botany out of doors, rather than from books alone. He learns his geography primarily by studying the school and the schoolroom, its environments, and then the city. He thus learns to read maps, and he understands things as you and I did not understand them at his age at all.

Ethics alone seem to be regarded as the exception. We apparently still think that we can develop the power of self-control without giving people freedom, that we can develop ethical power by merely talking about it, sermonizing about it. We still think that we can cultivate obedience to such an extent that it shall balance over and become self-control; and yet we know that living twenty years in prison, where the most perfectly enforced routine is secured, does not develop in the individual that high degree of self-control which such perfect obedience would suggest. The absolute obedience which the seamen on our men-of-war maintain during their ocean trips, where they rise on the minute, eat, work, play, attend divine service regularly, all according to well-regulated schedules, does not so establish within them that perfect self-control which will keep them from license on receiving shore leave in Yokohama, as I have seen. The seaman has not had liberty; so his free time does not mean freedom, but license—something which kills itself.

Time and again I have seen young men who had been cared for so assiduously by their parents as never even to choose their gloves, shirts, or neckties for themselves, whose funds had been so carefully administered for them that they themselves had no responsibility or freedom. They had, perhaps, been given small allowances to do with as they pleased, but all their essential needs were met. They never learned the value of money by having to earn it. They never learned the value of things by having to go without them. They never learned the necessity of control by having freedom, and thus learning by experience. And when these young men went to college and were given an allowance which should cover all their needs, they suddenly had an extent of freedom thrust upon them for which they were totally unprepared. It was just as if the baby had been compelled to wait with reference to controlling her bodily movements, so that she never fell or never even had the feeling of falling, until she was pretty well grown—until her desires were such as to lead her to climb to high things. She certainly would learn at some time the meaning of the fall, but at this later time the meaning might be disastrous; it might result fatally. So with these college boys. The expensiveness of learning freedom after one is well grown consists in the fact that the experiments involved are so large. The risks are so much greater, and disaster, rather than success, often results from such experiments in freedom at a later time.

The development of the ethical, social self must begin as soon as the child is old enough to have relations with other children of his own age, and it must continue as long as human life continues.

The relation of this to democracy is already evident. During our age we are witnessing an unparalleled development of commerce. Science in all its branches is progressing by leaps and bounds. The number of journals and books issued in the name of science has not only entirely passed beyond the capacity of Bacon's ideal, but the specialist in a single field—in a subsection of the field of physiology—cannot hope to keep up with the researches published in this line. So to know what is going on even in this one subject, one must take a section of a

254 A PHILOSOPHY OF PLAY

section of one science. The humanitarian developments of our times are unique and extraordinary. Our charity organization societies, the development of our hospitals, the wonderful "first-aid" work that is going on in the armies of the world, the relief work for children, the societies for improving the condition of the poor, the societies for sending destitute children to the country in summer—these are working in great numbers and with unprecedented efficiency. This is an era of popular education. Never before has so large a percentage of the population been in schools. Lectures for adults on improving subjects, correspondence schools, colleges, public schools, private schools—all mark a wave of interest in education that is new in the history of the world.

But we see also an unparalleled exploitation of the many by the few, with oftentimes a disregard for law. And further, we see a tendency for popular, unthinking, uncontrolled action, which is shown in its worst form by the lynch mobs. Both these tendencies are fatal to the permanent life of a democracy. These are two of the greatest dangers of our times—the exploitation of the many by the few and uncontrolled public action.

PLAY AND DEMOCRACY 255

Neither of these dangers rests upon the development of any new feelings in mankind, or upon the development of new intellectual or other powers. It simply appears that new opportunities have been given to old powers and that these enlarged opportunities consist in the nature of the material development which is now going on in the world. For example, the application of steam to transportation on land, railroads; to transportation on water, steam vessels; to printing; to all kinds of manufactures, construction, building, machine making, and the like, has made the modern city not only possible, but necessary. The modern city with its development of machinery places the emphasis upon elaboration rather than upon the production of raw materials. We are no longer, and can never be again, a farming, fishing, mining people. We must work where large numbers of persons can get together quickly, where commodities can be exchanged rapidly, where goods can be carried from one part to the other easily, where intercommunication is prompt, economical, and efficient.

Steam and electricity have tied the world together. They have made specialization inevitable, because they have created so many more things that need to be done. And thus has been vastly increased the mutual interdependence, not only of all people, but of all the peoples. It is not only true that the honesty of the banker in a community affects the welfare of the other people in that community; it is also true that the welfare of the farmer who supplies the milk, the butcher who furnishes the meat, the school-teacher who teaches the children, the city official—all these involve the welfare, or the reverse, of all the rest in that community. Communities are also mutually interdependent. A calamity to our great wheat-fields in the West would be a calamity for New York city, although we have no wheat-fields in the city. A financial calamity in New York would be a calamity to the wheat growers of the West—and wider even, a calamity to the wheat growers of America means a calamity to the bread eaters of the world. The mutual interdependence of all people has been increased, and it is this interdependence that has given opportunities for the great exploitation of the many by the few. This exploitation is in itself neither good nor evil. It may result in vast benefits to the community, as well as in benefits to those in control. The reverse may be true, but usually the two effects are mixed. So it is not any new human power that has produced

PLAY AND DEMOCRACY 257

these great dangers. They are attributable to the development of our material civilization, which has given opportunity for old power to show itself in new forms.

This interdependence has also rendered many things socially significant which in former days were largely individualistic. For instance, years ago, when our forefathers lived in small groups of families, the disposal of refuse was apparently a matter which affected the health of that individual family alone; other families lived far enough away so as not to be affected. The making of clothing by the family was not of social significance to the whole community as it is at present. Now clothing made in a home where there is scarlet fever is a menace to the entire community. A single case of typhoid in a family living near a stream may now result, and has resulted, in thousands of deaths in communities supplied with water from the same stream. This is possible only under conditions of water-supply as developed during city life. It is now a crime punishable by law to erect a wooden building within certain congested districts of large cities, because a wooden building is apt to burn, thus proving a menace to other structures. In the old days when buildings stood isolated, it was a matter of individual choice what materials should be used in construction.

So we see that in the matter of unthinking, uncontrolled action, it is not that we are less thoughtful and less controlled than in former days, but that we have suddenly had thrown upon us the need of self-control and thoughtfulness in a very large number of new directions. Conscience is growing as it has always grown, but the last century has seen thrust upon it a set of fresh burdens of an extent, complexity, and character unprecedented in scope.

These new deeds must be and are being met by changes in the direction of the development of conscience. Not that anything new in the nature of conscience itself is being evolved, but fresh subjects are being brought within its consciousness, fresh applications are being made of self-control. I refer to that self-control which is related to the very wide extension of the effects of one's acts as compared with former days.

That system of ethics, and the conscience that went with it, which was satisfied by the ideal of "visiting the fatherless and the widows and keeping one's self unspotted from the world," has passed. It is not enough to help the unfortunate of our immediate environment;

PLAY AND DEMOCRACY 259

the unit has enormously enlarged, until it embraces the whole community. Conscience is developing in civic directions and in corporate directions. We have not yet developed citizens in great numbers who possess a civic conscience, but we have some and more are coming. The last decade has seen an enormous development in the sensitiveness of conscience to corporate activity, and it is not too much to say that the conscience of our leading men is sensitive to corporate activities in a way that it was not ten years ago. It is no longer sufficient for a man to lead a personally blameless life in order to be socially esteemed in the community. His corporate life must not only be free from evil, but must have in it positive social good. It is no longer enough to pray and to work in accordance with the spirit of this plea, "Oh Lord, bless me and my wife, my son John and his wife—we four and no more"; because these four are so bound up with all the rest of the community that it is impossible to single them out either for good or evil. What affects them affects the rest. We stand or fall together.

These multiplex ties, the very ones that bind us in modern society, are the sources of a freedom that expands and gives us new power. We may have either slavery or freedom—depending upon the kind of people we are. If we can use freedom, we keep it. If we cannot use freedom, it turns into license and into slavery—not through the exercise of any external power, but in the very nature of the case.

The necessity of self-control and corporate civic conscience in a self-governed people may be illustrated by any number of historical cases. The failure of Liberia is an instance to the point. Here was a community built up of slaves who had grown up under conditions of autocratic control, who had not developed the power of using freedom, who had not evolved a social conscience, that kind of personal control which looks to the whole community for its effects. Liberia failed not because of the absence of ideals, but because there were not in the community enough persons who were accustomed to being free.

The story of the forty years' sojourn of the Jews in the Wilderness may not be literally true; it is, however, morally true. This group of former slaves had to be kept on the march, under the rigorous hygienic conditions of wilderness life for one whole generation, until there could arise a new generation that had been brought up under conditions of freedom. Then there was a measurable degree of self-control,

PLAY AND DEMOCRACY 261

and the development of property and higher social conditions could and did arise.

The difficulties that obtain in Russia to-day seem to be partly at least due to the absence of a sufficient number of persons who have learned the first lessons of freedom in childhood. There is no lack of passionate devotion; there is a lack of social control. Peoples of the world have certainly failed from many different causes, but prominent among them is their misuse of free time, that is, the time of their freedom—the misuse of that which gives the opportunity for the very highest development of the individual.

The type of freedom found in play is the type of freedom on which democracy rests. Is the boy free who is in a gang? In one sense he has very little freedom. If he does not wear clothes approved of by the gang, his clothes may be torn off. If ten members of the gang want to play ball, the remaining member is not free to go to the woods. If the others want to steal watermelons, he is not free to go home. His freedom is conditioned by the rules of the game and by the wishes of the group. This is the kind of freedom he may expect later in life; it is the only type of freedom which a human being, living in social relations, can hope to secure, freedom conditioned by rules and by the desires of others, expressed in law. This is the freedom of a democracy, and the control of a democracy is mutual-consent control. It is for this freedom and this control that play gives preparation and training.

Granted that the freedom from which alone self-control can come is one of the best gifts of play to our civilization, where shall we look for the other requisite of democracy, a sensitive social consciousness? In this respect, also, the playground has a tremendous contribution to make. Through the loyalty and self-sacrifice developed in team games by the mutual-consent control, we are laying the foundations for wider loyalty and a more discerning self-devotion to the great national ideals on which democracy rests. The gang instinct is in some respects anti-social, because the group is limited, but it marks the beginning of real social consciousness.

A great play festival was held in Chicago in 1907. Large groups of the various peoples of that city came together and presented their national dances, expressing the ties that bound them to their own pasts and uniting with other citizens in a spirit of civic unity. It was an occasion of great significance in the welding together of diverse elements of our nation.

The immigrants coming to America have frequently been made to feel that their past was not wanted. The smart young American has not understood the traditions of the country from which his parents came. He has failed to understand the significance of their national and folk-dances, the historic traditions which help to tie the individual in a community to that which is wholesome in the past, as well as to express that which is necessary in the present.

The need of developing a new country has taught us the necessity of work. We have yet to learn the place of play and recreation— not as individuals, but as social units—for we do not live as individuals, but as parts of a social whole. These folk-dances and games in which many individuals can participate afford one of the few avenues that exist for the expression of mass feeling. The spirit of unity has been developed as much by these exhibitions of common feeling as by the mere fact of working together. Working together in some industry or factory may instil into the coworkers a kind of unity or sympathy; but the getting together on an occasion of freedom where they can express their joy in a symbolic dance operates far more effectively in bringing about this consciousness of the whole.

Some years ago, at the instigation of a committee, the Greeks of Chicago presented "Ajax," an old Greek play. The effect upon the Grecian workers of the city was astonishing. They came to be conscious of themselves as a people. It was not merely a performance done for the enjoyment of others; it was a recognition of their common historic past and of its tie with the present. It is not by chance that the peoples of the world have developed their dances and other means for celebrating occasions. We Americans need these occasions also, for we are built of the same stuff as are the other nations. Celebrations of this type are not merely entertaining; they meet a deep need that we all feel—the need for community action. The time will surely come when every city will have developed its own celebrations, when those holidays that belong to all in common shall have acquired an art form in which they may be adequately expressed.

Democracy must thus provide not only a seat and instruction for every child in the school, but also play and good play traditions for every child in a playground. Without the development of the social conscience—which has its roots in the early activities of the playground—we cannot expect adults to possess those higher feelings, which rest upon the earlier social virtues developed during childhood. The sand pile for the small child, the playground for the middle-sized child, the athletic field for the boy, folk-dancing and social ceremonial life for the boy and the girl in the teens, wholesome means of social relationships during adult life—these are fundamental conditions without which democracy cannot continue, because upon them rests the development of that self-control which is related to an appreciation of the needs of the rest of the group and of the corporate conscience that is rendered necessary by the complex interdependence of modern life.

CHAPTER XX
PLAY, THE PURSUIT OF THE IDEAL

JACOB RIIS told the story of a little sick girl who had been hungry a long time, and who did not have sufficient clothing to protect her from the biting cold. Some good friend who discovered her asked what more than anything else she would like to have. She replied: "Can I have just what I want?" "Yes," was the answer. "What I want," said the little girl, "is a pair of red shoes."

There are things in life more important than bread. To that little girl red shoes meant beauty, the thing desired, the ideal. Many persons who have been in the cold without sufficient clothing, food, or shelter, because they possessed the things of life that for them were ideal, have been happy and have lived wholesome lives. The reason for the coarseness and sordidness of the great mass of people is not their lack of sufficient food, shelter, and clothing. It lies in the fact that they have not been successful in the pursuit of other than material things. Or

THE PURSUIT OF THE IDEAL 267

quite possibly it lies in the fact that they have not even pursued these other aims. They have had no ideal which meant more to them than comfort. They have been driven by necessity, not by desire.

Play is what we do when we are free to do what we will. It is the spontaneous expression of the inner desire. A father came home one day and found his nine-year-old daughter writing busily. Face and hands indicated extreme tension and severe labor. He asked her what she was doing, and she replied: "Please don't disturb me. I am doing something very important. I am on the entertainment committee of the Saturday Afternoon Club, and I am writing the programme." It was finally produced as follows:

1. Praise God from Whom All Blessings Flow.
2. My Country, 'Tis of Thee.
3. Waltz.
4. Come Ye That Love the Lord.
5. Two-step.
6. I Need Thee Every Hour.
7. Love Divine, All Love Excelling.
8. Hark! the Herald Angels Sing.
9. Irish Dance.
10. Spanish Dance.
11. Where Is My Wandering Boy To-night?
12. Barn Dance.
13. God Be With You Till We Meet Again.

Here was the human spirit expressing itself freely, fully, like a field flower. Fortunate, indeed, are they who retain this spirit for manhood and womanhood—adding only work! Religious feeling, play, and work—a balanced life. We labor now magnificently, but the two other avenues of expression die young. Another age may have to expend its best energy in getting us back to dance, pray, and play.

The work which the world counts really great has been done in this spirit of free self-expression, which is also the spirit of play. The poems of the world, the great statues, the great paintings of the world—these are not produced under compulsion. The *Portuguese Sonnets* were not a product of economic necessity. One cannot conceive of the work of Rodin being produced because of the need of the money which it brought. While he was doing the work into which he was putting his life, he was supporting himself by laboring in a factory where images are made for the trade; but his life interest lay in the pursuit of the ideal. That is the contribution by which the world remembers him. The famous violin-makers, who loved their instruments and could hardly bear to part with them, worked because they enjoyed it. They were not impelled by necessity, but by desire.

THE PURSUIT OF THE IDEAL 269

I talked with a tool-maker in Pratt Institute, and as I picked up a two-part tool that he had just made, I said:

"How closely does it fit?"

He answered: "I don't know"; but he added that it fitted closer than one-thousandth of an inch.

I said: "Why can't you tell?"

To which he replied: "I have no calipers that will register closer than that."

I said: "Is it necessary to fit it so closely?"

"No," he said, "it is not."

I said: "Why do you do it?"

Then he just looked at me. That man's work was his life. He was expressing himself as did the old violin-makers; he was pursuing his ideal. It was not the lash of economic necessity that was driving him, nor the scourge of public opinion.

That is what I mean by play, and that is what play really is. It is not something less than work. It means a difference in mental attitude. One may play when ploughing, or cooking, or experimenting, or reading poems—or one may work. One attitude is the pursuit of the ideal; the other is a mere acceptance of the compulsions of life. Play as a matter of fact slides over into what is called work, but the glorious thing about life is that usually the great work is play. Not only the work which becomes famous may be done from the standpoint of play, but all work that is worth doing. The teacher who loves to teach, the business man who is fascinated by "the game," the inventor who forgets sleep because of interest in that which he is bringing into the world, the mother who does her tasks with joy born of love for her children—all these are acting from desire. They are expressing themselves freely; they are playing.

When a boy has rigged up a little paddle-wheel in the stream in the meadow and has devised a way by which a thread may be attached to the axle and a small block of wood hauled up against the current, he has done essentially what Edison does when he has been evolving a new electrical attachment. In the absorption of the occupation he has forgotten all about his meals; everything else has become of no consequence; the enthusiasm and joy of a certain ideal have taken possession of him. That is play. It is the spontaneous enlistment of the entire personality in the pursuit of some coveted end. We are not compelled to pursue this goal; we wish to pursue it, for it is our main desire. In the light of it everything else—dinners, punishments, the world's opinion—become inconsequential. We have not taken possession of the idea; the idea has taken possession of us.

THE PURSUIT OF THE IDEAL 271

Play does not mean the omission of difficulties, or even of hard labor. A boy playing a game may work harder than he could possibly be made to work by any other means. He may not enjoy all the details of the play, the training for athletic sports, the hard practice, the defeats. But he accepts them because he has chosen the game; and he knows that the game involves rules. He will submit to the rules because they are necessary for the end he desires. Similarly, a man who does his work because of desire will submit to endless detail and routine if it is necessary for the accomplishing of the work. It is not drudgery, forced upon him from an external group; it may be hard, it may be wearying; but it is that which he himself has chosen to do. He does it because he wishes to do it, and for no other reason.

This play attitude may be deliberately assumed in the face of the tasks of life. A boy who was compelled to work in the wood-shed showed his imagination by pretending that the blocks of wood were Indians whom he was attacking. The difference in attitude made the whole difference in the enjoyment of the work. Two sisters who had been quarrelling in their play were suddenly heard to say: "Let's play sisters." From that time on they played harmoniously, fulfilling their ideal of the sisterly relation.

There was a difference between being sisters and playing sisters: in the first case the condition was imposed, in the second case the relation was a chosen one, an ideal to be worked out in action. Kipling has given classic expression to this joy in work for the work's sake in his "L'Envoi":

"And no one shall work for money, and no one shall work for fame;
But each for the joy of the working, and each, in his separate star,
Shall draw the Thing as he sees It for the God of Things as They Are!"

The phrase "Art for art's sake," although it has become distorted from its original meaning, had this idea back of it, that any work worthy of being considered æsthetic must be done for the joy of the process. The attitude of play can be taken deliberately under much less promising circumstances than those in which the artist is situated. Many adults, compelled to do tasks which seemed in themselves uncongenial, have quite consciously done as the small boy did with the logs in the wood-shed; they have made a game of their work. This is possible even under difficult conditions, and it usually requires much less mental effort to stimulate desire than to do the work from the sheer heave of duty and with a dissenting spirit.

THE PURSUIT OF THE IDEAL 273

The way in which the feeling of the game may be taken into the affairs of life, giving power and the ability to endure to the end, has been stirringly expressed by Henry Newbolt, in a poem describing how the spirit of the cricket match saved the day for a British regiment on the battle-field.

"There's a breathless hush in the Close to-night—
Ten to make and the match to win—
A bumping pitch and a blinding light,
An hour to play and the last man in.
And it's not for the sake of a ribboned coat
Or the selfish hope of a season's fame,
But his captain's hand on his shoulder smote—
'Play up! play up! and play the game!'

The sand of the desert is sodden red—
Red with the wreck of the square that broke;
The Gatling's jammed and the colonel dead,
And the regiment blind with the dust and smoke.
The river of death has brimmed its banks
And England's far and Honor a name
But the voice of a schoolboy rallies the ranks:
'Play up! play up! and play the game!'

This is the word that year by year,
While in her place the school is set,
Every one of her sons must hear
And none that hears it dare forget.
This they all with a joyful mind
Bear through life like a torch in flame,
And, falling, fling to the host behind—
'Play up! play up! and play the game!'"

That is what life is, at its highest and best—a playing of the game, a pursuing of the ideal under the rules and limiting conditions necessary for this pursuit. The pursuit is an end in itself. The goal of life is not found in any definite acquisition of pleasure; and, curiously enough, children do not play for pleasure. The boy does not say: "It will give me pleasure to play marbles." He says: "I want to play marbles." He does not think of the pleasurable state of feeling that will occur when he secures a jackknife. He thinks of the knife and wants it. It is only the sophisticated person who says: "It will give me pleasure to eat these grapes." The ordinary person thinks of the grapes and wants them. Pleasure comes with the eating, but rarely abides in consciousness as something to be sought. We do not choose because of the pleasure; we choose because we have the desire. Desire and not pleasure is the ultimate motive.

The real satisfaction of life is not found in any end that is attained. One of my children made a doll's house with a very complete set of furniture, with pictures on the walls, a piano, a bed and bedclothes. She seemed possessed with the desire for a doll's house and worked at it intensely from early morning until late at night. But

THE PURSUIT OF THE IDEAL 275

she did not want the doll's house when it was completed. At that moment her satisfaction in it began to lessen. The doll's house was not the real end. A man worked with great enthusiasm over the logical structure of logarithms, sitting up all night to learn it. He thought his motive was that he wanted to use that particular knowledge later. But he never cared to use it afterward; his joy was in the accomplishment, not in the thing acquired. Boys will work for hours or days to make a house or a wagon, and their satisfaction wanes the moment the object is completed. It is a common experience for men to set a mark beyond which they will not go in the earning of money. But that mark is passed again and again, and still they keep at their work.

Our minds are so constructed that they draw curtains over past achievements. We are not satisfiable beings. Choice is not to be regarded as existing for the sake of any definite content of pleasure, nor for the end to be attained. We want something and get it, and at once it is behind us. So long as we have it not, we long for it, and our hearts go out after it. We use every feeling of earnestness and passion for its attainment, and then when we get it, it is gone from our desire and we strive for some other thing.

The essence of choice is not in the end, but in the choosing. In the doing is the result. Happiness is not in the attainment, but in the attaining. "Life is in the quest."

President Hadley has drawn attention to this fact, that we are moved by the splendor of the action rather than by the tangible results. "Turn back over the pages of history to the stories that have most moved men's hearts, and what are they? Stories of action, deeds of daring, where the risk habitually outweighed the chance of practical results. Nay, the most inspiring of them are often manifestations of hopeless bravery, where the likelihood of success was absolutely nil. When we read of the soldiers of Gustavus Adolphus's regiment at Lützen, who after the loss of their king stood firm in their ranks until the line of the dead was as straight as had been the line of the living on dress parade; when we hear of the *Cumberland* at Hampton Roads waging the hopeless fight of wood against iron, and keeping the flag afloat at the masthead, when the vessel and all who remained in her had sunk; when we remember the tale of the Alamo, in whose courtyard and hospital a handful of American frontiersmen fought the army of Mexico, without hope of victory, but without a thought of retreat or surrender, till they earned by the very completeness of their annihilation the glory of that monumental inscription: 'Thermopylæ had its messenger of defeat; the Alamo had none'—then do we see how hollow is our pretense of valuing things by results, when we are brought face to face with the really heroic struggles of life. It is the doing that makes the deed worthy of record, not the material outcome."

The first conclusion to be drawn from these facts about human choice and free play is that life, self-activity, is an end in itself. This is true all the way up the human scale; it is as true for the child as for the adult. The man who is willing to brush aside the child's feeling about play, thinking of his activities as mere preparation, completely misunderstands the nature of human life. That child is now living the human life, his feelings are the same and the results of living are the same to that child as they will always be. Though the process be with purely imaginary objects, though the child be making an imaginary currant jelly with an imaginary dish on an imaginary stove, the process is real. And the process is an end in itself. The impulse to play is the impulse to express oneself, to function, to live. We make great slaughter of our own and our children's lives when we think of ourselves or of them as preparing to live. Life is now; the present process is the real end of desire and of choice.

Simply because this is a real process, not an imaginary one, is there a succession in desires. The nature of the desires that hold us through life, that make us endure pain, that keep us joyously at our tasks, varies with our development. There is a constant conflict of different desires. The boy wants to play, but he also wants to eat. He wants to please his mother, and he wants to please himself. The man wants to hunt, but he also wants to succeed in business. There is a conflict, and the nature of the man will determine whether he shall leave his business and go hunting, or give up hunting and keep to his business. These purely egoistic desires remain in some form throughout life. The joy of skill in manual work belongs to this group of pleasures.

This conflict is constantly renewed on a higher plane. There is tremendous joy in competition; the boy's whole life is poured out in the passionate desire to win. But certain forms of fighting must injure boys who are friends of his. The old desire to fight his chum may give way to a new desire to stand by him. There is a higher pleasure in self-sacrifice for those whom we love

THE PURSUIT OF THE IDEAL

than there is in competition with them. If the man grows wholesomely, he will come, at last, to have a love for his city, his country; he will work and sacrifice for it, not from a sense of duty, in the unpleasant use of that word, but because he wants to, because he loves his city. He has the same kind of feeling of satisfaction in service that the little boy had in building blockhouses. He is doing it from an inner impulse, from the stress of desire.

Desire is a greater word than duty. It is a fine thing to do right when one does not wish to do right; but it is a finer thing to desire the right. It is a mother's duty to care for her child. But the mother who stays awake at night, who sacrifices herself for her sick baby just because it is her duty, is living on a low level compared with the woman who does all this and more because she wishes to do it, because she loves the child. The man who "does his duty" to his wife never does his whole duty. I knew a man who noted in his pocket memorandum certain days when he would take flowers to his wife. He regarded it as a married man's duty to pay these attentions to his wife just as he had done before marriage; so at stated and regular intervals he purchased flowers. But the highest expression of life loses its chief value if it is done from a sense of duty; the highest expression of life must be one of desire.

The growth of personality is shown by the change in the things we desire. One day my twelve-year-old daughter came to me for a talk. She had noticed, she said, that the girls of thirteen and fourteen in our neighborhood had stopped playing with dolls, and had also stopped "hitching" to grocer wagons and other vehicles. She said: "I have made up my mind that I am going to 'hitch' until I am eighteen, and I am going to play with dolls until I am twenty." She also fixed some other dates. I replied: "Why do you make up your mind about it? Why not just do it as long as you want to?" She answered: "I want to until then. I know I shall want to until then. But it will be a little hard, because the other girls will stop doing it, and I shall have to do it alone." She was giving almost perfect expression of the state of mind in which many of us face the joys of life. We hold on to them; we are afraid to let them go. We want the present maintained in the future, not realizing that the present joy may be a stepping-stone to a larger one. But just as the baby enjoys playing with his toes, and that joy serves its turn and passes into the background of consciousness to make

THE PURSUIT OF THE IDEAL

room for greater joys made possible by greater powers, so for adults this constant progression is not only possible but necessary for the fullest life.

We must go forward to new joys and new activities as spontaneously and gladly as a child goes forward to new plays. When we have reached adult years, and have become self-conscious in our joys, the new truth may hurt at first. Even the small boy is hurt by the discovery that there is no Santa Claus, unless this discovery comes to him in connection with a larger truth. The youth who learns that the earth is not flat and that the world is merely a speck in the universe, may feel miserably small for a few days. The greater truth has not yet made its way. And the world has ostracized and killed those who brought new truth to it. The fear of losing the present good is a natural fear, but it may be overcome by the conscious realization of the fact that the process of life is continuous, that the new is built upon and perfects the old, that, as Browning has said in his "Rabbi Ben Ezra," "The best is yet to be."

INDEX

ADULT:
  Play, 113
AESTHETICS:
  Feeling, produced by smoke, 54
  In house play, 73
ALTRUISM:
  Man's, developed through tribe, 89, 98
  Team games, altruism from, 150, 194
  Woman's, developed through home, 93, 97
ANGLO-SAXON:
  Play, xi, 147, 154, 162
ANIMAL:
  Play, 99
ARITHMETIC:
  Teaching of, 180
ART:
  Play impulse in, 268
ASTRONOMY:
  Interest in, 172
ATHLETICS:
  Boy character shaped by, 91
  Discipline of, for women, 97
  Origin of, 28, 90
  Track, interest in, 188
  Womanliness and, 92

BABY:
  Climbing attempts of, 243
  Girls' love for, 79
  Play of, 184
BASEBALL:
  American game, 197
  Interest in, 1, 3, 4, 171, 239
  Money spent on, 114
  Origin of, 198
  Speed of, 163

BASKET-BALL:
  Woman's reaction to, 84, 89, 93, 97
BEAR:
  Hunt, in tribe play, 205
BEAUTY:
  Desire for, 266
BERLIN:
  Play of small children in, 14
BIRD:
  Instincts, 104, 111, 200
  Interest in birds, 172
"BLACK MAN": 16
BLACKBIRD:
  Instinct to sing of, 200
BLOCK:
  City, for play, 228
  Play with blocks, 69, 225
BOAT:
  Construction, 68
BODY:
  Control in play, 149
BOSTON:
  Playgrounds, 7
BOXING: 22, 29
BOY:
  Exercise of small, 156
  Gangs, 194
  Imitation of, 208
  Initiation ceremonies of, 202
  Subnormal, 128
  Unrestrained, 207
BUILDING:
  Blocks, 71
BULL FIGHT:
  In Spain, 22

CAMP FIRE GIRLS:
  Fire ceremonies of, 64

INDEX

Cat:
  Game of, 4
  Play of, 100, 106
"Cat's cradle":
  In Borneo, 241
Census:
  Play, 113
Character:
  Development from continued abode, 43
Chicago:
  Playgrounds, 7
Chicken:
  Chirping of, in egg, 99
Child:
  City, opportunities of, 229
  Defective, in school, 168
  Home life of, 220
  Initiation of savage, 201
  Institution, play of, 137
  Life in play, 277
  Older, play space for, 13
  School life of, 217
  Small, play space for, 13
  Subnormal, 128
  Work of, with parents, 214
Church:
  Grounds, use of, 227
City:
  Craps, a city game, 238
  Life, and the individual, 257
  Life, and shelter feeling, 43
  Modern industrial, 255
  Play in modern, 224, 228
  Populations, 212
Civilization:
  And play, 211
Club:
  Boys', 5
Community:
  Action, 264
  Interdependence of communities, 256
  Play, 222
  Traditions carried by, 237
Competition:
  Boys' plays characterized by, 83

  Early play and, 149
  Middle life and, 188
  Morals, effect of competition on, 189
  Origin of, 90, 187
  Women's, 97
Concentration:
  Children's, in play, 12
Conflict:
  Life a conflict of desires, 278
Conscience:
  Civic, 258
Construction:
  House, 38
  Ownership and, 67
Continuity:
  Affected by city living, 43
Control:
  Body, in early play, 148, 185
  Mutual consent, 206, 245, 247, 262
  Play, 206, 232, 240
  Playground, 230, 244
  Self-, and democracy, 265
  Self-, and obedience, 251
  Social, 254
Cooking:
  Fire play, 50
  House play, 5, 39, 45
  Social significance of, 46
Co-ordination:
  Feeble-minded, co-ordination of, 131, 133
  Muscular, through rhythm, 136
  Neural, in throwing, 84
  Neuro-muscular, early in life, 185
  Play, from simple to complex, 153, 165
Courage:
  Fighting plays, and, 30
Craps:
  A city game, 238
Cricket:
  English football, 197
  Fighting, 21
Curriculum:
  Kindergarten play, 182

INDEX 285

Play, 175
  School, 176
CUSTOM:
  Social, from shelter feeling, 40

DANCE:
  Folk, in America, 236, 242
  Folk, for feeble-minded, 136
  Folk, at play festival, 262
  Hall, evils of, 121
  Hall statistics, 115
DEMOCRACY:
  Play and, 243
DESIRE:
  Feeble-minded, lack of desire of, 128, 133, 135
  Great achievements, desire present in, 180
  Knowledge, desire for, 183
  Life motive, 266
  Play characterized by, 127, 177
DOG:
  Fighting feeling in, 201
  Hunting feeling in, 111
  Play, 102, 105, 106, 110
DOING:
  Joy in, 274
DOLL:
  Boy's reaction to, 83, 86
  Girl's reaction to, 85
  Play, 74
  Social value of, 94
DULUTH:
  Playgrounds of, 231
DUTY:
  Desire greater than, 279

EATING:
  Social, relations of, 46
EDUCATION:
  Home, passing of, 217
  Physical, of feeble-minded, 136
  Play and, 171
  Popular, 254
ELECTRICITY:
  Interest in, 173

ENDURANCE:
  Play, endurance learned in, 163
ENERGY:
  Absence of, in feeble-minded, 132
EPOCH:
  Culture, play theory, 141
ETHICS:
  Freedom and, 249, 251
  Modern, 258
  Playground, 245
EXALTATION:
  Play, 19
EXAMPLE:
  Play, 234, 239
  Power of, 219
EXERCISE:
  Boy's, aged four, 156
  Boy's, aged two and a half, 157
EXPERIENCE:
  Learning by, 243
EXPLOITATION:
  Present-day, 254, 256

FALLING:
  Lessons in, 243
FAMILY:
  Development of, from shelter feeling, 41, 42
  Life, change in, 215, 219
  Relations through doll play, 78
FARM:
  Work, 215
FATIGUE:
  School, 176
FEAR:
  Feeling of, in play, 16
  Fire, 56, 58
FEEBLE-MINDED:
  Play of, 129
FEELING:
  Domestic, centred on doll, 69
  Fire the symbol of, 63, 65
FESTIVAL:
  Play, Chicago, 262
FIGHTING:
  Instinct in terriers, 201
  Interest in, 143

INDEX

Literature, fighting in, 22
Plays, 16, 29, 83
Prize, interest in, 1, 21, 23
FIRE:
  Camp Fire Girls' use of, 64
  Fear, 56, 58
  Play, 49
  Religious significance of, 60
  School fires, 248
  Social significance of, 61
  Symbol of feeling, 63
FISHING:
  Interest in, 6, 142
FOLK DANCE:
  See Dance.
FOOD:
  Play. *See* Cooking.
FOOTBALL:
  Interest in, 2, 171, 188
  Player, interest in, 208
  Soccer, 197
FOURTH OF JULY:
  Celebration, 116
FOX:
  Play of, 106
FREEDOM:
  Ethics of, 251
  Play, 208, 245
  Use of, 259
FRIENDSHIP:
  Establishment of, 144
FROEBEL:
  Play theory, vi, 182

GAME:
  Carrying of game traditions, 204
  Development of games, 235
  Fascination of, 125
  "Playing the game," 195, 273
GANG:
  See also Tribe.
  Authority, 261
  Boys', origin of, 38
  Danger of, 245
  Instinct and development of, 90, 194

GENEALOGY:
  Interest in, 173
GEOMETRY:
  Study of, 175
GIRL:
  Little sick, 266
  Work of, in home, 216
GROWTH:
  City, 212
  Moral, and play, 184
  Play an indicator of, 133
  Play in relation to, 152, 155
  Time for, 181
GUIDANCE:
  Play, 195, 199
GUINEA PIG:
  Play of, 105
GYMNASTICS:
  Fatigue of, 157
  Inadequacy of, 162
  School, aim of, 168
  Undue demand in, 176

HABIT:
  Formation of, 182
HADDON, DR.:
  Cat's cradle in Borneo, 241
HEREDITY:
  Social, 202
HOARDING:
  Instinct of, 80
HOLIDAYS:
  Celebration of, 236
HOME:
  Authority in, 249
  Changes in, 216
  Development of, 92
  Feeling, through fire, 53
  Feeling, in house play, 33
  Loyalty to the, 89
HOUSE:
  Building, with blocks, 73
  Doll houses, 75, 78, 274
  Playing, 33
HUDSON, W. H.:
  Play of pumas, 101

INDEX

HUNTING:
  Bear, in tribe play, 205
  Feeling, 5, 20, 142, 145
  Feeling, in animals, 111
  Plays, 16, 83
  Statistics, 20, 114

IDEAL:
  Play, the pursuit of, 266
IMAGINATION:
  Stimulation of, 72
IMITATION:
  In education, 180
  In play of feeble-minded, 134
  Unconscious, 208
INDIAN:
  Tribes of Mr. Seton, 205
INDIVIDUALISM:
  In play of feeble-minded, 130
  In play of young children, 148
INDUSTRIALISM:
  Growth of, 212, 220
INDUSTRY:
  Development of, in home, 92
INITIATIVE:
  Play, lack of, in city children, 139
INSPECTION:
  Medical, of school children, 168
INSTINCT:
  Animal, 199
  Animal, developed in play, 110
  Blind, unreliable, 210
  Domestic, development of, 94
  Gang, 90
  Maternal and paternal, 87
  Play, 177, 197, 205
INSTITUTION:
  Children, play of, 137
INTEREST:
  Children's, significant for education, 155
  Development of, 171
  Pulses of, in play, 145, 164, 175
  Pulses of, in work, 174

JAMES, WILLIAM:
  Flying instinct in birds, 104
JUSTICE:
  In competitive period, 189
KINDERGARTEN:
  Plays of Froebel, vi, 182
KIRK, ADRIAN:
  Play attitude in work, 125
KITE:
  Play, 151
LADDER:
  Play, 225
LAW:
  Developed from shelter feeling, 40
LEADER:
  See also Teacher.
  Play, 140, 233, 239, 242
LEADERSHIP:
  Play, 12
LEISURE:
  Use of, 119
LIBERIA:
  Failure of, 260
LIFE:
  Modern changes in, 212
  Play attitude in, 271, 274
  Reality of, in play, 179
  Social, through doll play, 76
  Social, through eating together, 46
  Social, and the individual, 257
  Social, through ownership, 81
  Social, through team games, 91
LOCALITY:
  Feeling for, 43
LOVE:
  In literature, 22
LOYALTY:
  Group, 91, 190
  Sex differences in respect to, 88, 97
  Team, development of, 150
MANLINESS:
  Athletics test of, 92

INDEX

MARBLES:
  Play, 146, 150, 162
MILLS, WESLEY:
  Play life of animals, 102
"MONKEY CHASE": 235
MORALITY:
  Fighting plays developing, 30
  Freedom and, 250
  Home and, 217, 219
  Play and, 184
MORGAN, LLOYD:
  Chirping in eggs, 99
MOVING PICTURE:
  Evils of, 122
  Statistics, 115
MUSCLE:
  Development of, in city, 167
MYSTERY:
  Fire, 58

NATURE:
  Interest in, 144
  What is "natural," 209
NERVOUS SYSTEM:
  Stress upon, in city, 166
NEW YORK:
  Defective children in, 168
NEWBOLT, HENRY:
  Poem by, 273

OBEDIENCE:
  Absolute obedience, non-moral, 251
  Necessity of, 247
OTTER:
  Swimming of young, 201
OWNERSHIP:
  Construction and, 67
  Feeling, development of, 79
  Feeling, in fire, 50
  Feeling, in house, 39

PARIS:
  Playgrounds, 232
PARK:
  Grounds, use of, 227

PARTY:
  Doll, social significance of, 78
PAWTUCKET:
  Playgrounds, 231
PERSONALITY:
  Desire and, 280
  Development of, by doing, 74
  Ownership and, 81
PHILANTHROPY:
  Development of, 254
PLAY:
  Adult, 113
  Anglo-Saxon, 147, 154
  Animal, 99
  Attitude in life, 125, 271
  City, 224
  Civilization and, 211
  Community, 222
  Curriculum, 175
  Definition of,
    xii, 11, 99, 124, 125, 126, 179, 267, 269, 270, 277
  Democracy and, 243
  Direction and control, 230
  Education in relation to, 171
  Extent of, 1, 6
  Fair, 190
  Forms of, 9
  "Free," 232
  Froebel's theory of, vi, 182
  Function of, 124, 169
  Greek, "Ajax," 264
  Leadership, 12
  Life in relation to, 10
  Masculine and feminine differences in, 83
  Moral growth and, 184
  Movement, 7, 8
  Progression, 141
  Pulse of, 70
  "Pursuit of ideal," 266
  Reason for, 116
  Seasonal rotation of, 150
  Subnormal children, play of, 128
  Team, 191
  Team, of girls, 89

INDEX

Theories, 90, 116, 117, 182
Tradition, 235
PLAYGROUND AND RECREATION ASSOCIATION OF AMERICA: 8
PLAYGROUNDS:
Boston, 7
City, 230
Chicago, 7
Movement, 8, 9
New York, 123
Pawtucket, 231
Statistics, 8
Toledo, 230
Unsupervised, 122, 230
Well-managed, 244
Yard, 224
PLAYHOUSE:
Twenty-storied, 33, 227
PLEASURE:
Not life motive, 274
POPULATION:
City, 212
POWER:
Increased, source of enjoyment, 186
PROGRESSION:
Play, 142, 162
PROPERTY:
Development of, from shelter, 40
PULSE:
Play, 70
PUMA:
Play of, 101

RACE:
Habits, community, play related to, 110
Habits, play reverting to early, 118
REALITY:
Feeling of, in play, 179
RECREATION:
American, unorganized, 222
Different from play, 123
Necessity of, 119
REFLEX:
Acquiring of, early in life, 185

RELATIONSHIP:
Human, on playground, 249
RELIGION:
Fire used in, 59
Home, passing of, 217
RHYTHM:
Use of, for feeble-minded, 135
RIGHTEOUSNESS:
Social, establishing of, 193
RIIS, JACOB:
Story by, 266
ROOSEVELT, PRESIDENT:
Statement about free play, 232
ROTATION:
Seasonal, of plays, 150
RUNNING:
Interest in, 26

SAND:
Bank, for fire play, 49
Pile, 14, 225
Play, of adults, 148
SAWING:
Wood, at University, 211
SCHOOL:
Children, defective, in New York schools, 168
Children's life in, 221
Curriculum, 176
Fires, 248
Growth of, 217
A monarchy, 248
SCIENCE:
Development of, 253
SELF-EXPRESSION:
In play, 170, 177
SELF-MASTERY:
In early play, 148, 185
SEPARATION:
Of children in play, 12
SETON, ERNEST THOMPSON:
Indian tribe, play of, 205
Play of foxes, 106
SEX:
Differences, in play, 45, 83
Differences, in shelter feeling, 34, 38

290   INDEX

SHANTY:
  In wood, 33
SHELTER:
  Feeling, 34, 40, 143
  Feeling, racial differences, 41
SKATING:
  Roller, 228
SLAVERY:
  And freedom, 260
SMOKE:
  Aesthetic effects of, 54
  Religious significance of, 60
SPECIALIZATION:
  Growth of, 213, 255
SPEED:
  Progression, in play, 163
SPELLING:
  Teaching of, 180
SPONTANEITY:
  Play, 130
STORY:
  Ghost, effect of, in firelight, 58
STREET:
  Play of children in, 221
STRIKING:
  Origin of, 26
SUPERVISION:
  Institution playgrounds lacking, 138
  Necessity of, 230
  Play, 206
SUPERVISOR:
  See also Teacher.
  Play, 233
SURVIVAL:
  Theory of play, 90
SWIMMING:
  Learning, 176
SWING:
  Playground, 224
SYMBOL:
  Doll used as, 77
  Fire, 63

TAG:
  See also Running.
  Games, 16

Origin of, 26, 28, 187
Small children's, 185
Universality of, 238
TEACHER:
  Rôle of, in play, 71, 195, 222, 240
TEACHING:
  Instinct of, 209
TEAM GAME:
  Of feeble-minded, 130, 134
  Origin of, 90
  Social significance of, 91
  In teens, 191
  Woman's lack of team play, 93
TENNIS:
  Interest in, 188
TERRIER:
  Scotch, fighting instinct in, 201
THEORY:
  Culture—epoch, 141
  Play, a balance for work, 116
  Play, a return to the simple, 117
  Play, survival, 90
THROWING:
  Interest in, 23, 27
  Learning of, 149, 174
  A masculine interest, 84
TOLEDO:
  Playgrounds, 230
TOOL-MAKER:
  Ideal of, 269
TOYS: 67
TRADITION:
  Animal play, 111
  Feeble-minded play, 134
  Gang, 204
  School, 203
  Social, in play, 89, 177, 189, 197
  Social, passing on of, 202, 218, 237, 263
TRAINING:
  Physical, in schools, 168
TRIBE:
  See also Gang.

INDEX

Gang, the modern tribe, 92
Loyalty to, 89
TRUANCY:
Cause of, 178
TWAIN, MARK:
Play attitude of, 125

URBANIZATION:
Increasing, 212

VITALITY:
Developed by play, 166

WILL:
Deficiency of, in feeble-minded, 133
WOMAN:
Work of, in home, 217

WOMANLINESS:
Athletics no test of, 92
WOOD:
Sawing at University, 211
WOOD-SHED:
Need of, 67
WORK:
Artistic, is play, 268
Children's, with parents, 214
Joy in, 272
Moral lessons of, 179
WRESTLING: 29

YACHTING:
Statistics, 114
YARD:
Playground, 224

Brenda Nevitt

©2015 by Red Chair Publishing

ISBN Number: 978-0-9967651-0-7

All rights reserved.

No portion of this publication may be reproduced in any form without written permission from the author.

Names of some individuals have been changed out of respect for their privacy.